For the l

Marla J. Selvidge

Roseville Publications
a Division of
Loch Lloyd Travel Consultants, LLP
(Cover Design by Marla J. Selvidge)

Copyright © 2014 Marla J. Selvidge

All rights reserved.

ISBN-13: 978-0-9895808-2-3

The image of Elvis Presley used in cover design
was created by Martin Charlot.

It is a detail taken from his mural "Stars in Paradise" found at the Consolidated Theatre in Kahala, Honolulu Hawaii. Copyright ©1995 by Martin Charlot.

Email address: martindaycharlot@aol.com

DEDICATION

For Laura M. Scott, Ph.D. who cheered me on as
I researched and wrote this book.

Also, for "Sonny" who shared her love for Elvis with me.

CONTENTS

Acknowledgements
Forward
Introduction, 2

1	Elvis Achieved the American Dream	13
2	Elvis Was Just a Normal Guy	29
3	Elvis Was Generous	46
4	Elvis Loved his Family	57
5	Elvis Was an Innovator in Music	68
6	Elvis Was an Early Adapter of Technology	92
7	Elvis Lived on the Edge of Traditional Morality	98
8	Elvis Trusted People	114
9	Elvis was a Southerner	127
10	Elvis Loved His Fans	137
	Appendix	146
	Resources	147
	Author Page	158

ACKNOWLEDGMENTS

Many thanks to Colette Tilden, Sonny, Igor Yusov, The Chrysler Corporation, the Lbrarians for Elvis Presley Enterprises, Martin Charlot, Elvis Presley Enterprises Australia, Thomas C. Hemling, Cindy Valla, Wendy Hawkins, Sarah Craig, Lisa Schmidt, Albion Mends, Gersham Nelson, the Interlibrary Loan Wizards at UCMO including Vanesa Chappell; and the College of Arts, Humanities, and Social Sciences at the University of Central Missouri for supporting me in the research on Elvis and travel to Graceland. Special mention should be made regarding the scores of people who encouraged me with their interest, humor, and personal stories about Elvis. What a journey this has been!

Forward

The thoughts you will find in these pages are a humble attempt to capture the profound, and lasting significance of Elvis. There are thousands, if not millions of fans, who probably know more about Elvis than I do. I have not spent the better part of my life as a fan. All the same, after reading and studying Elvis' life and music for three years, I was compelled to write about the Elvis I discovered! The global canon of literature dedicated to exploring Elvis is enormous. My resources were, unfortunately, all in English.

This tribute represents a serious yet positive attempt to analyze the impact and career of Elvis Aaron Presley. Some of the photos in this work may make you smile, and this might lead a reader to discount the academic quality of some of the comments and theories because those images are included. Most academic books would not include humorous images. For me, photos of memorabilia capture the sweet and funny side of Elvis.

The notes engulfed all of us. You never forget that kind of uplifting musical experience!

There were other points of contact between my family, Elvis, and me. Every morning we listened to "hillbilly" music on the radio. Now, later in life, I am so surprised when I listen to the Country-Western songs and Elvis' songs of the time. I know all of the lyrics. Did I hear those on the radio? My mom and dad's radio looked something like the image below!

Elvis listened to the radio too because most people did not have television sets in the late 1940's and early 1950's. Radio connected people to the world. The more I read about Elvis, the more his early life paralleled my mom and dad's life. Both were born in rural areas, mom was from Holly Hill, Kentucky and dad grew up in Soddy, Tennessee before it was linked with Daisy to become Soddy-Daisy. His great claim to fame was a lot of his earlier records. Like every other junior high girl, I played, "I can't help falling in love with you," over and over but it had nothing to do with Elvis. I faintly remember that it was a big thing when he came home from the Army. But other memories are sketchy? I was working my way through college (three jobs) and did not even own a television, so I missed the big 1968 Comeback Special and all the news about him. (Recently, I have gone through boxes in my basement and found two 45's of Elvis songs and two albums dated from 1976 and 1977. So I must have been a mini-fan!)

When I was about eight years old, our entire family watched Elvis perform on the Ed Sullivan Show. My parents loved him. After all, he was from their part of the world. I never understood the complaints I heard from some that Elvis was doing "evil," because we danced our brains out to all sorts of music that copied the Chuck Berry style. I even hung out with friends who played in a dance band. What did Elvis do? Beats me! We were already shaking everything in my town!

Dang, I wish I had saved the tickets. In 1976 I was there and so was Elvis. He performed a concert in Greensboro, North Carolina. It was like a host of angels singing with Elvis who was leading them in a white jumpsuit. He was not as slim as I had recalled but it did not matter, the concert and songs were earth shattering.

"Elvis. An Afternoon in the Garden," that I had picked up at a Best Buy for $4.99. We like to listen to different types of music when we are rolling from one campsite to the other. I had not listened to or thought about Rock n' Roll for decades. Elvis' songs we were playing were lively and uplifting. The exact moment that we crossed the Oklahoma border (no lie), Elvis was belting out, "I've never been to heaven, but I've been to Oklahoma." Tom and I burst out laughing. No one could have predicted that Elvis would be singing about Oklahoma just as we crossed the border. It was a sign!

Another vivid sign came one early morning as I was driving to my office at the University of Central Missouri. Since our vacation, I had purchased a few other CD's of Elvis' music and was listening to "I'll be home on Christmas Day." All of a sudden I heard "tones" that I remembered in my father's speech. My father died about five years before Elvis did. He had been raised near Chattanooga, Tennessee, not far from Memphis. There was an unexplainable connection with this song!

I remember listening to Elvis when I was a kid living just outside of Detroit, in Roseville, but was not a fan. People like Bobby Darin and Marilyn McCoo, Billy Davis Jr., and Tony Orlando were at the top of my list. Motown was my center of attention. I loved folk music too with John Denver, the Mamas and the Papas, as well as the Everly Brothers. Bob Dylan was not even in my site. I danced to Elvis music but don't remember owning

Introduction

It Happened To Me Too!

"He captured my heart."

Cheryl Skogen, an Elvis Fan

Our 2009 Fleetwood Motorhome

There he was, in my life, and he was not going to go away, but it happened thirty-five years after Elvis had left us. Chugging down Highway 69 in Kansas after a full day's visit at Ft. Scott in our Fleetwood Motorhome, we inserted a CD of Elvis songs, standing outside the courthouse in Dayton, Tennessee and listening to what he called, "The Monkey Trial." The Scopes Trial was decided in 1925 when my father was only 13 years old. They argued a case as to whether evolution should be taught in public schools.

If Elvis' life and career had not been such a great moment in history, none of us would know about his personal habits. According to several sources, Elvis did not like taking a shower or a bath. He had his hair washed by a hair-dresser and preferred what the old folks call a "foot bath." He hand-washed himself with water in a bowl, say some. Kathy Westmoreland says that he smelled like "Neutrogena" and took showers just like everyone else. She has no idea how this myth about Elvis began. (Westmoreland, 217)

Our home in Roseville, Michigan did not have a shower. We had a bathtub. Most of the time we only took a bath once a week. The rest of the time we followed hand washing like the kind attributed to Elvis. While Elvis ate banana and peanut butter sandwiches, we did not. We could not afford the bananas. Peanut butter was given to us by people down the street who were on welfare. It did not taste very good and came in gallon metal containers. Mom usually threw it out! I think it was raw peanut butter without any sugar? She offered us Wonder Bread sandwiches laced with Kraft Miracle

Whip. There was little nutrition contained in those meals!

Just like Elvis, my father would take jelly and hard margarine in a plate and mix it together and then place it in globs on a hot biscuit or toast for breakfast. I could not stand the sight of him doing it because he had more hard margarine on his fork than jelly. I often wondered if this was a meal he ate when he was young and without any food. There was so much margarine!

Of course on Sundays we ate fried chicken with hog-gravy and mashed potatoes, green beans steeped in pig hocks, and sometimes sauerkraut. We also ate pinto beans with fried corn bread. My mother loved to eat crisp fried corn bread placed in a glass of buttermilk for breakfast. Like Elvis' diet, my mom and dad's diet was unhealthy. They ate too much bacon, fried crisp of course, sugar, biscuits and gravy, and not enough vegetables or fruit. And we loved ice cream, and lots of it! We pretended our kitchen was a soda fountain just like Elvis did almost every Friday. On Friday's when dad got paid, he would stop at the A&P grocery store and buy a pint of chocolate Sealtest ice cream. We split it among all of us.

The sweet tones and links with Elvis inevitably led me to read about his life, loves, great work, and personal challenges. After listening to many, many albums of rockers and popular music during the 1960's and 1970's, not one even comes close to the range and abilities of Elvis. (Of course many may disagree with me, and I will admit that I am biased.) I also listened to Johnny Mathis for years, but he does not have the heart and soul of Elvis. There are many great and creative artists, but their voices or interpretative abilities are not a match. Elvis touches all of us because he was one of us, and we will explore his extraordinary humanity in the remainder of this book.

Perhaps the one place that touched me the most while visiting Graceland this year was seeing the grave of Elvis, his parents, his twin brother, and his grandmother. I had a sense that the myth I was reading about actually was a real person.

Peter Townsend, guitarist of the British rock band "The Who," said, "A man that changed my life at the age of eleven. I saw Elvis Presley live at eleven. Thank God I did, I loved him..." In Townsend's song, "Real Good Looking Boy," he compares himself to the beautiful boy Elvis and comes up short." His mother said that he was an ugly boy but that she loved him all the same. Elvis inspired him to pursue his love of music, which created a career that has lasted over forty years. (Real Good Looking Boy)

Elvis has inspired me too. His life mimics "freedom" and I think I have gained a touch of that in my life because of studying him. Becoming a full professor is a long and arduous journey and I have appreciated achieving that rank. But, now, later in life, I view it as a straightjacket. When they say that you study a "discipline." That is exactly what you do; you become an expert in the field of your choice. But by limiting yourself to your "discipline" you must leave out many other interesting things in your life. Elvis pushed a button for me that has changed my view and direction in life.

I define what I do in this book as "Elvisology." "Logos" or "logia" is the Greek word for "study," so we will be studying and pondering Elvis. My research is based upon what I term the "witnesses of the life of Elvis." It is amazing that so many of the books about Elvis written by those so close to him are so similar. They seem to focus on the same topics of sex and drugs. Some of their abilities to understand and articulate the "real" Elvis were very limited because of their backgrounds and lack of learning experiences in life.

In this book I try to theorize about a lot of issues surrounding Elvis and differ with many of those eyewitnesses. I often wondered if they did not understand the language of Elvis. They kept trying to translate it into something they understood, but I do not think that many of the witnesses ever really understood or appreciated the genius of Elvis. Like many writers, these books project their own image of themselves and highlight their own accomplishments, rather than accomplishments by Elvis. And we must note, as we do later, that these books were written by hired writers who interviewed the "witnesses."

Each of the following chapters will answer the question, "Why do we love Elvis?" Later, I will give you instructions and an opportunity to tell your own story and, perhaps, have it and your photos included in a following book on Elvis. See the Appendix.

A display of Elvis collectibles at Graceland!

"The young man with the ancient eyes and the child's mouth, a body as loose and unadorned and as unpredictable as a whip.... In the eye of the hurricane the young man took it all with unnatural good grace and humility....

But after a year, there were no more clothes to buy; there was no more good food to be wanted; there was no room for more Cadillacs or motorcycles; the home appliances were all bought and paid for; the future was assured; Mom and Dad had nothing left to desire, for they had all they could ever use...."
(Dundy, 270)

Chapter One

Elvis Achieved the American Dream

"But money isn't everything...."

"Just because you're poor doesn't mean
you're white trash, even if you're a sharecropper."

Billy Smith   (Nash, *Baby*, 3)

Compiled photos of Images in Sonny's Collection

Elvis has become a symbol of freedom to all people who are bound by their environments, their birth, their education, and their regionalism. For some he has become an American God.

(Strausbaugh, 24) In 2014, we have come out of our own great depression. Millions of people lost their jobs and thousands of college graduates could not find work. Factories were closed, pensions were seized, and states stood on the edge of bankruptcy. Some cities, like Detroit, began cutting the pensions of its retired workers.

People who had owned fabulous homes and lived incredible lives, found themselves sleeping in their cars and showering at a local YMCA. Homeless and hungry children could not go to school. They moved around too much. African-Americans, Latinos, and light-skinned males seemed to bear the brunt of the recession in the United States. The wealthy have recovered and are financially soaring after the recession but the other segments of society keep losing wealth. Some people call this the "two Americas."

Elvis was a member of the "other" America. He was born in 1935 into abject poverty only a few years after the 1929 stock market crash. Of course he did not understand the full extent of what it meant to be poor as a child. None of us understand that we are poor until we experience how more affluent people live. My mother was seven years old when the stock market crashed. She said that if it crashed, it did not affect them. They never heard about it. In fact, it seemed like a boom to her because all of a sudden there were jobs with the Civilian

Conservation Corps that paid real money. Her family did not have much cash because they grew most of their food, dug coal for heating and cooking out of the mountainside, hauled timber for kindling, and traded for other things they needed. And even though the CCC was in town, my mother had to share a pair of shoes with a sister. Her best clothing was created out of used flour sacks.

Elvis knew that times were "rough," especially when his father was sent to prison. He knew his dad worked for the Civilian Conservation Corps just like my grandfather, Joe Gilreath. He knew he had to live with relatives. He knew he did not have a bed of his own. He knew that he did not have indoor plumbing. He knew that he did not have enough to eat. Yet, he still may have not viewed himself as disadvantaged. In order to understand how disadvantaged you are, you have to have an experience of those who are "advantaged."

Elvis remembered his roots every day of his life. In spite of his wealth and popularity, Elvis was a very humble person. "You have to know how it is to be so poor, to never be able to go to the movies or to have things you want, to know how really wonderful it is to see and have a few things...." (Mann, 17) "I was nine when we went to Memphis to see our relatives, and I discovered a bathroom inside of a house! I was amazed." (Mann, 19)

Even when his family moved to Memphis, there was

not enough money. On dates with young girls or hanging out with buddies, he borrowed money so he could eat. He worked after school, sometimes taking full-time jobs. And most of us, when we were young, had to find a job too if we were going to have good shoes and clothing. My mother took me to Suburban Drugs to meet Mr. Eid, the owner of the store, (about a mile away from our home) when I was only fifteen. She negotiated a job for me delivering prescriptions. (I had been babysitting up to six children since I turned ten. That money paid for my clothing, a bedspread, and drapes for my bedroom.) But I was too young to have a license to drive a car. I kept making excuses to Mr. Eid until I finally got my license at 16.

Elvis watched both of his parents struggle to survive. He wanted something better and promised them that he would take care of them. His mother loved Liberace and later in life Elvis even dressed like him. He wanted to please his parents but most importantly, he wanted to take care of his "babies," as he called them. As a teenager he took the lead and became the chauffer for his parents. (Dundy, 91).

Many of us had or have similar dreams of taking care of our parents, siblings, or other family members. As a child I found myself explaining things to my mom and dad who had not graduated from high school. My two brothers were placed in my care when I was only eight years old. I carried my brother around with me when he was a baby. That close relationship lasted until I left home at seventeen. And as an adult, I supported my mother for at least forty years. I remember that my mother always wanted to buy my brother and me an ice cream from the Good Humor man, but she could rarely find a dime anywhere in the house. Often, when he drove down our street, she could find a nickel and we would split a dual-stick popsicle. She never had enough money to buy an ice cream for herself.

Elvis did not spend his entire career working in a factory, or slaughterhouse, or even collecting garbage like so many of our parents and us. But Elvis did work in a factory, Marl Metal Products, for a while. And in 1953, he worked at Precision Tool for about $1.25 an hour. Elvis did everything he could to earn money. He mowed lawns, helped to deliver bread for the Wonder Bread man, sold concessions at special events at Ellis Auditorium, and worked as an usher in a theatre.

According to Guy Coffey, at Ellis Auditorium, "Elvis would sell Cokes. He would get a small percentage of what he sold. On a good night, Elvis would earn three or four dollars. That may not sound like much nowadays, but then, to a kid from Humes, living in Lauderdale Courts it was a fortune. Sometimes, after the night's event had ended and the Hume's kids had settled up, financially, Elvis would go up on the stage and play (his little guitar) to imaginary crowds, bowing to their applause." Years later Elvis would entertain on that same stage. (Burk, *Early Years*, 129)

A long time ago after landing my first good paying job, I said to my mother, "My hard work has paid off, I am going to make decent money." She came back at me and said, "Honey, a lot of us have worked just as hard or even harder, and it never paid off for us." My mom worked in an automobile or airplane factory most of her life. Elvis understood the hopelessness that people feel when they are stuck in a monotonous job. He knew how difficult it was for his parents, and he had been stuck all of his early life. People work and work and work and yet, they don't seem to be able to make a living wage. They are always juggling one payment with another or one prescription with a utility or food bill. They can't relax because another bill is waiting around the corner and they don't want to be living in a shanty or worse.

After graduating from high school, Elvis went right to work as a truck driver. He admired truckers. Perhaps he dreamed of driving out of town and experiencing the world. A truck could take you anywhere. You did not have to live in one place. I know a career trucker in his seventies and he still has to get out and go. Staying in one place makes him feel claustrophobic. Yet, silly dreams of entertaining people filled Elvis' head. He wanted to be a singer and an actor. Elvis remembers those days to May Mann, "I know it looks like I came up overnight. Not so! I can tell you it was a lot of hard work. I've done plenty of it. I worked as a common laborer, up at three every morning to work in a defense plant; I drove a truck for Crown Electric in Memphis, the same thing I was [doing] in high school. I'd get out [of school] at three-thirty and be on the job at six-thirty for $12.50 a week ushering in a movie house." (Mann, 9) (Someone sent this copy of a Social Security card to me. I don't know if it is real or not.)

SOCIAL SECURITY
ACCOUNT NUMBER
409-52-2002
HAS BEEN ESTABLISHED FOR
Elvis Aron Presley
WORKER'S SIGNATURE
FOR SOCIAL SECURITY PURPOSES • NOT FOR IDENTIFICATION

Elvis wanted to play football. Many books suggest that Elvis would not cut his hair for the team. This is another one of those myths that cast a negative light on Elvis' life. According to the football coach Rube Boyce, Elvis never had any money for lunch, and so he took a job so he could eat. (Burk, *Early Years*, 101) That job interfered with football practice. Elvis also considered joining the boxing team. Walt Doxey, the coach, placed Elvis "in the ring against Sambo Barrom," who became one of the most successful boxers in Memphis. Sambo bloodied him good. Later, Elvis returned and explained to the coach, "I am a lover ... not a fighter." (Burk, *Early Years*, 121) Somehow Elvis managed to find enough money to buy a ROTC uniform and wore it often. He was very proud of the association and the discipline that he learned. (Burk, *Early Years*, 101)

Fannie Mae Crowder Caldwell, of Memphis, remembers Elvis well. "The Presleys were living on Alabama and my sister was living above the grocery store down the street. The house the Presley's lived in was really just a shack. It had three rooms and they did not even have a toilet in the house. They had an outhouse. After he started appearing on the Louisiana Hayride, I heard one night he ordered eight hamburgers. They thought he was kidding, but Elvis said, 'No, I never had any money to buy hamburgers when I was growing up, so I want eight now.'" (Burk, *Early Elvis*, 79)

There is something about living in a southern family that brings people together. Family means everything. Relatives are more important than friends. My mom and dad never went to the movies or concerts and rarely socialized outside the family. Vacations away from Roseville, Michigan were spent visiting relatives in Kentucky and Tennessee. If we were going to socialize, it was with family. Dad was a Mason, and early in his life with mom, he attended meetings but that stopped.

Occasionally they played cards with the neighbor next door.

Southerners know that there are different castes of people, those who are inside and those who are outside the family, especially if you live in the north. Outsiders never learn about family secrets or treasured thoughts. They normally did not experience delicious southern dishes like fried corn and okra and sweet potato pie, or quilting, and canning all the vegetables you need for the winter. And as much as Elvis loved people, he also was afraid of outsiders as a boy, according to several accounts (Mann, 15).

Elvis' first opportunity to win wealth came one day in 1954 when he sweated out, "That's Alright Mama," with Scotty Moore and Bill Black at Sun Records in Memphis, Tennessee. Sam Phillips made it happen. He was only nineteen years old. Spinning that record on a local DJ show one evening began the trek towards his dreams. The Blue Moon Boys were formed.

First they played and sang locally and then with whirlwind speed, they toured the south. Elvis worked very hard. He knew that fans were bread and butter for him. He gave the shows everything and sometimes ended up being taken to the hospital after fainting from exhaustion. That happened again, later in life, when he passed out after a show at the Gator Bowl. (Guralnick, *Last Train*, 254) They sang every day and night if they could. Pay was small and mostly only covered their travel and expenses. Scotty was the manager and even approached Tim Diskin, Tom Parker's assistant to help with bookings. He was turned down. They kept on playing the smaller joints, making very little money.

It was not until 1956 when Elvis signed a contract with RCA records for $40,000 that a down payment on Elvis' dreams was realized. Federal Minimum Wage at the time was $1.00 an hour. Even if you double the minimum wage, people could work an entire year for $4200. Elvis was paid only $40 a week in 1954, or about

$2000 a year. In 1964 at my first job, I was only paid $.75 an hour in 1963 (the minimum wage in 1954) so my pay was below minimum wage. I did not know it. Forty thousand dollars was a vast sum of money for the average person.

By 1957 Elvis had purchased Graceland for his parents. He was only 22 years old. You can find many sites on the web and read books about his net worth or income, but who has studied all of the records? Sean O'Neal in his 1997 book, *Elvis Inc.*, estimates that Elvis earned $4 billion in his lifetime and Elvis Enterprises, Inc. had earned $4 billion since his death. He gives an example of one year in Elvis' career, 1965. Elvis earned over $5 million, yet his net after paying his manager, his agent, and the IRS was about a million. His manager earned a net $1.3 million. Vernon, "a man with a seventh-grade education" managed Elvis fortune and his incompetence with taxes and investments cost Elvis $100 million (O'Neal, 5-20).

Photo taken at Sun Record in 2013. Sam Philipps and Elvis Presley

But we know the stories about people who have won the lotto! Achieving the American Dream can be a nightmare. "The National Endowment for Financial Education estimates that as many as 70 percent of Americans who experience a sudden windfall will lose that money within a few years. People handed a hefty check also usually experience erratic emotions ranging from elation to resentment to anger, according to the NEFE." (Lottery Winners) People hound you for money and your life may change drastically. Jealous people may have you killed for your new fortune.

Graceland in 2013

Elvis kept winning the lotto (so to speak) year after year, and also found himself in a very difficult situation because of his wealth and popularity. Among those who knew him and those who pretended to know him, there is a common thread of jealousy. Elvis needed friends, but who was his equal? Those closest to him misunderstood him and hated the time he spent with books and questions about life. Priscilla, his wife, even convinced him to burn his treasured books. It was like burning his friends. They all wanted his money, fame, and attention.

Books were probably his saviors in the midst of so many people who lived from one moment to the next. Many people misunderstood him or manipulated him for their own selfish ends. They forgot his genius and talent because they focused on their own petty concerns. Some, like Albert Goldman and the boys, scandalized his life for money or to enhance their careers

Others, who were banned from his tours, earned money for the rest of their lives by lecturing and meeting the fans in the name of Elvis. They claimed he was their buddy. Even his family controlled the marketing of Elvis in order to enhance the wealth of the estate. He was an object to be used, a victim of his own success. Tom Parker commented, "Elvis isn't dead. Just his body is gone." (Nash, *Mafia,* 731) Lamar Fike, a high school buddy of Elvis who traveled with him for years made a comment about the death of Elvis that is very revealing, "Elvis's death fucked up everybody's life. Most of us weren't trained to do anything but look after him." (Nash, *Mafia*, 737) In many cultures throughout history, when a king dies, his servants are buried with him. Lamar's words ring true.

Lamar should have taken care of his own life. He was too passive to search out and create a long-term competent career for himself. He chose to ride the flame of a star. Long before Elvis died, Lamar had decided to ruin his own life but, in the end, blamed it on Elvis. He claims, "Every one of us is exactly like Elvis in some way." (Nash, *Mafia*, 762) No, they were not like Elvis. This is a dream. They so identified with him that they became him, but they never had the talent or abilities of Elvis. They never could do a mind meld with him; their minds would have exploded.

Yet the question lingers, "Why did Elvis choose to keep those types of people around him?" From my point of view, I think that he was a good-hearted person and wanted to save the world so he saved a few people he knew by employing them. But there must be some other reason? Perhaps they reminded him of his former life, a life that may have made him happier than his current life? Maybe he just liked them, or maybe he found people who were willing to become what he needed? Maybe he thought of them as the brothers and sisters he never had?

Yet, we all know that by the end of his life, Elvis had realized his dreams many times over. His life gives hope to others that they, too, can scramble out of poverty, if only they dream and are willing to make the sacrifices and put in the very hard and punishing work that Elvis did in order to achieve his goals. Thank you, Elvis!

From Sonny's Collection

"There was magic in that voice -- but there was magic in those ears, too. I was blown away at how Elvis would shape not just his own performance, but the entire track.... [A]lthough he didn't take credit often, I believe Elvis is the most underrated producer in rock and roll." Jerry Schilling (Schilling, 143)

Chapter Two

Elvis was just a Normal Guy

"He [Elvis] knew that he was powerful only when he sang."
(Dundy, 125)

Elvis, like most of us, was not a Rhodes Scholar, neither did he attend Oxford University. Kris Kristofferson who finally accepted the lead role in "A Star is Born," which Elvis was offered, had obtained both. Elvis had graduated from high school because his mother wanted him to graduate, otherwise, he would have gone on driving a truck.

When Elvis entered the Army in 1958, he took several exams and did not score high enough to take the officer's examination. (Hopkins, 192) People often use these tests to argue that Elvis was just a country hick with no brains. Yet, today, we know that all tests are culturally biased. And questions often reflect the cultural upbringing of the people who create them. I was recently told a story by an African-American professor that black children in one school district were scoring very low on national exams. For instance, students were asked what color is a banana? The correct answer is obviously yellow. But if you are a child who lives on the desperate edge of poverty, you might answer "black," because that is the only color of banana that you eat, the black ones, and the over-ripe ones that no one else will eat.

I took an IQ test in elementary school. My teachers told me that I was not college material and that I should find manual work for a career. Could it have been a cultural bias since I was raised in a southern family? How wrong they were! How wrong the test was, because I earned a Ph.D. early in life and became, among other things, a college professor. Tests predict something, but I really don't know what they predict because they cannot predict the innate ability and drive or determination of a person. And so it was with Elvis. If he had stayed in the military, he would have eventually reached the top post.

Elvis was just a regular guy who liked to have fun, friends, and physical exercise. He always invited people to join him in the evenings or after a concert. As an only child, perhaps he liked having people around him all of the time. He played sports like football and worked very hard to master Karate so he could defend himself. During most of Elvis' life, people did not exercise very much. Jack La Lanne had a show on television that emphasized physical exercise, but most people thought those big muscles he had were ugly. You didn't need to exercise to keep healthy or live a long life. Of course, most people were wrong. Now our health providers tell us to be active every day of the week.

Elvis liked automobiles. They were not just to look at but also to drive, and he loved to drive. He loved the movies and firecrackers on the fourth of July and all of those women who followed him everywhere. He also loved to read. According to Dr. Nick, he carried trunks of books with him when he traveled. In the second edition of this series, we will discover the exceptional mind of Elvis. Elvis also liked to eat and later in life to fly, fly anywhere. He would have loved to have flown to Japan and toured all of Europe, but that did not happen.

He also loved jewelry and fine clothing. A jeweler often traveled with Elvis so that Elvis could purchase gifts in a moment's notice. Elvis created symbols that he had transformed into jewelry for all of those around him. His mind never stopped and his creative juices were always flowing. They were powered by his kind and gentle heart.

Elvis feared and loved the public at the same time. Early in his career he had had his clothing ripped off of him, his automobiles defaced, and fans had stormed the stage on which he was performing and smashed the instruments. Toward the end of his life when he was receiving threats of assassination, he learned how to shoot a gun to defend himself. He became a collector of guns. He wondered why anyone would want to kill him? Kathy Westmoreland, a soprano and friend of Elvis', says that Elvis got so upset that he said, "I can't believe it! Why would a guy want to kill me? I've been so upset that I can't even go to the bathroom." (Westmoreland, 41) Stressors were many in the life of Elvis. There were paternity suits that never panned out. Even after his death, no one has proved that he or she is a child of Elvis.

Elvis was a dreamer. In accepting an honor by the Jaycees in 1971, he said, "When I was a child, ladies and gentlemen, I was a dreamer. I read comic books and I was the hero of the comic book. I saw movies and I was the hero in the movie. So every dream I ever dreamed has come true a hundred times." (Schilling, 223) Like so many others, Elvis escaped boredom and his economic circumstances through his imagination.

The guy who became the sex object of millions of females in the twentieth century could not dance, according to Charlie Fisher, one of his high school buddies. "Funny thing, when he's on stage he does all that shakin,' but he can't dance with a girl because he does not know how to dance." (Burk, *Early Elvis*, 75) This makes sense to me. While Assemblies of God

(Elvis' church) or Pentecostal Churches allowed dancing for the Lord, they frowned on dancing in public. Dancing could lead to drinking and other things that were controlled by the devil.

It also makes sense, because Elvis was a non-traditionalist. He did not want to fit into acceptable parameters of social living, so why would he want to learn to dance? Luther Nall, another high school friend, emphasizes that Elvis was an individual. He was not swayed by peer pressure. "Elvis, even in those days, was a very sensitive, very compassionate person. He was an individual, no doubt about that.... Elvis was a very strong-willed person. His real ambition was steered by compassion and caring, not fame and fortune." (Burk, *Early Elvis*, 69)

Elvis allowed himself to be drafted into the military. There were several avenues that would have allowed him to perform concerts or to obtain a waiver because he was the only child, but he did not take them. He chose "to do his duty" and do what most males in the United States wanted to do at the time, serve their country. Although he was not placed in harm's way, he did have to clean cars, chauffer superiors, and work like any other military person on a base. He lived off the base to protect himself and to have a private life. He proved that he had the ability and discipline to "make it" in the military. He was proud of those years and the people with whom he served.

Elvis, although handsome, was frail in many ways. His bones ached. He had toothaches and cluster migraines. He got depressed. Often he felt very alone before and after a concert. He tended toward excess at times in both food and purchases for his friends and for himself. Some say that he disliked the movies in which he acted so much that he would become sick before shooting began. Jerry Schilling, a younger friend who eventually traveled with Elvis, quotes Elvis, "I cared so much until I became physically ill. I would become violently ill.... At a certain stage, I had no say-so in it. I didn't have final approval of the script, which means I couldn't say, 'This is not good for me....'" (Schilling, 244) To him, the scripts were all the same story, even though the actors and sets changed. Take a whirl through many of his first movies and discover the biased and bland plots.

Some time during his later concert tours, Elvis developed glaucoma. Glaucoma is a swelling of the eye that leads to inscrutable pain and blindness. Check out the sunglasses that Elvis began to wear because light bothered him so much. At one recording session, he was in so much pain that he was taken to a hospital where a doctor told him that he had to insert a needle into his eye to take off some of the pressure. If he did not do this, Elvis would go blind in one eye. Speculations about his eye problem blame it on hair dye, make-up, bright lights at concerts, and genetic predisposition. He was diabetic, and the two problems go hand-in-hand.

And Elvis was lonely. This is probably true of anyone who is at the top or is so creative or intelligent that no one around them really can converse with that person. According to Kathy Westmoreland, "He was surrounded by superficial thinkers..." "His interests were so varied and so widespread and he pursued his studies so intensely that I felt sorry for him living in a gold fish bowl environment without much freedom to do what he wanted." (Westmoreland, 35) Kathy believed that if Elvis had not been a singer and performer, he would have become a physician.

Elvis was vulnerable. According to Sam Phillips, "He tried not to show it, but he felt inferior. He reminded me of a black man in that way; his insecurity was so markedly like that of a black person." (Guralnick, *Last Train*, 43) According to Elaine Dundy, a biographer, Elvis was an outsider when he was very young. "For the children did not love Elvis. They would hear him sing and their hearts would fill with emotion.... It was the song they loved, not the singer." "The element of ridicule that surrounded Elvis all of his life had begun early.... We used to laugh at Elvis in sixth grade because he didn't have a front porch on his house--and he still doesn't." 'He was never in the wealthy "in" group but stayed within the amorphous "out" group among high school students who had little money and no political influence in town."

(Dundy, 123)

During his career, Elvis surrounded himself with buddies from high school, the military, and close family members. He created his own village. But Elvis was also very loving and generous. There are hints in a number of books that those around him played him for whatever they could get from him. It was a contest and then they would trade the things that were given to them. They were jealous of people who received gifts outside the village and wondered why some people received things that were worth more than others. Elvis trusted these people with his life and they knew it. Many times he would give a gift of a car, or a home, or a mobile home and the people would not keep the gift. They would sell it for the money. He knew that he had to keep them happy but toward the end of his life he could no longer give as much as he wanted to give.

Some of his life-long friends/bodyguards had beaten up so many people under the pretense of protecting Elvis that Elvis could not afford the bad publicity or legal costs to protect them. Kathy Westmoreland takes on those who bad-mouthed Elvis and calls their words "untruths" or "lies." They later attacked him in a salacious book. They continued the trend of bad-mouthing Elvis. They bit the hand of the person who loved them for decades, and perhaps, it facilitated his early death. These vultures lived with him, and then used his body for nourishment after his death. It is a sad tale of the American dream gone badly.

Like every star, Elvis had to have a hairdresser. His natural hair was blonde but he preferred it black. So he had to dye his eyebrows also. No celebrity buys clothing off a rack and certainly not Elvis. Bill Belew and Gene Doucette created all of his clothing, including his touring outfits. Elvis often came up with themes for the jumpsuits.

In a recent trek through Nebraska and South Dakota, we discovered Buffalo Bill Cody and his "Wild West Tours." It is interesting to compare Elvis' white jumpsuits with the white buckskin outfits that he wore. The similarities are so startling that I wondered if Elvis or his designers had studied his life. Stenciled on both of their outfits are nationalistic and Native American themes. Buffalo Bill, like Elvis, brought two different races together. While some of his tactics are questionable, Bill introduced the Lakota or Sioux Native Americans to thousands of light-skinned people.

Elvis and Bill seemed not to have a grain of prejudice in their bodies. While other light-skinned men were calling Native Americans savages, he was studying with them, training with them, and creating ways for them to earn a living. (I suppose you could argue also that he took advantage of them.) In Nebraska you can visit his home where he built a place called Scouts Rest Ranch.

Here is where Native Americans came to stay and rehearse for another on-the-road show.

Jackets worn by Bill Cody.

Detail of one of Elvis' jumpsuits at Graceland.

Additional clothing worn by Elvis.

Elvis had a lot in common with Marilyn Monroe. Both had to maintain their beauty and sex appeal. Elvis felt that he had to be perfect. Check out his photos as a child, then early in his career, and then his "1968 Comeback Special." Notice his nose. Notice his sculpted face. On more than one occasion Elvis had plastic surgery on his eyes, his nose, and perhaps more.

Lamar Fike, tells the story about how when Elvis was very young, Vernon dreamed the house was on fire and picked up Elvis and thought he was throwing him out the window. He was actually throwing him against the wall. You wonder about the injuries he sustained from that throw. Throughout all of his life, Elvis walked in his sleep, as both of his parents did. (Nash, *Mafia*, 27)

Elvis loved to wear makeup to enhance his face. There are many stories about how Elvis would go on a

Jell-O diet just before a tour. He was on one the night he died. Parker and his Hollywood cronies wanted Elvis to look thin in the movies. Parker's wife would even hug Elvis around the waist to determine if he had put on weight.

There is a lot of evidence that models who starve themselves for their career ultimately, end up destroying their health that cannot be regained later in life. Obviously, Elvis followed in the footsteps of starving himself periodically. Reports say that he went through many regimes to lose weight. One of them involved placing him in a hospital and keeping him in a coma-like suspension for three weeks, called a sleep diet created by Dr. Elias Ghanem. Elvis did the coma thing two times in order to lose weight even though other physicians advised against it. (Schilling, 275, Nash, *Mafia*, 669) He might even have taken hormones.

Lamar Fike, who weighed at least 300 pounds, had bypass surgery on his colon in order to lose weight. He lost weight until he got down to about 170 pounds. Elvis paid for the surgery but eventually Lamar had to have the surgery reversed because he was dying. He was not getting enough nutrients and his body was falling apart. Lamar died of Lymphoma in 2011. While no one has ever indicated that Elvis had this surgery, I often wonder about his weight. He seemed to be smaller in a couple of later films. In the movie, a *Change of Habit*, he looks like a stick. His waist could be no larger than 30 inches. And if he did have this surgery, it may have contributed to the decline in his health.

As noted, early in his career Elvis was very active and experienced threats of kidnapping. But as he aged, those activities began to slow. Elvis liked a physical challenge so he began studying Karate. During breaks in filming he would demonstrate his ability to break boards, but those stunts wound up giving him broken fingers and, perhaps, damaged vertebrae in his back. Look closely at his hands in some of his photos and you will discover gnarled fingers. Football was another way that Elvis let off steam and he could have sustained life-long injuries here. He played hard and sometimes got hurt, although friends claimed that they protected him when the heat was on.

Even with all the money he earned, life for Elvis was very challenging. He saw many doctors and asked for advice often. Insomnia, migraines, and a spastic and dysfunctional colon that would not evacuate waste plagued him in later years. Like his mother, he had liver disease caused by pernicious anemia that has no cure. Today, perhaps these problems could be alleviated or suppressed because the health care system has progressed so much.

Some of the latest information I have read about Elvis suggested that his sheets would be full of blood when he got up in the morning. Some suggest that he threw up in the night and others that his colon bled. It could also have been a vessel broken in his prostate? There are several reports that Elvis had leukemia and or bone cancer just before he died. He complained of gross pain in his hands especially. At times he could hardly walk. Kathy Westmoreland, Dr. Nick, Charlie Hodge and Elvis' father believed that he had bone cancer. And Larry Geller said that he had Leukemia.

What does it mean to have bone cancer? The answer is very different today than it was forty years ago. My Uncle Joe Baird had a form of bone cancer. It took him years and years to die of it. It was very painful. Every year we would visit him and he would shrink a little bit more. The last time I saw him before he died his rib cage had sunk down in his body over his waistline and he could no longer walk.

Even toward the end of his life, when Elvis was retaining fluids and had little energy, he continued singing. It is painful to watch him attempt to perform in the last documentary of his life, *Elvis in Concert*. Perhaps if he had taken the time to rest, to have an operation on his colon, and to exercise more he would still be here with us today. But then there is that nagging issue of bone cancer? Yet, he chose to work, to sing, to greet the fans and experience their adoration until it was over.

There are those detractors, even his own family, who claim that Elvis was addicted to prescription drugs at the end of his life. Ed Parker, a karate instructor and protector of Elvis, Kathy Westmoreland, and Charlie Hodge, a friend of Elvis, and Dr. Nick, his physician deny that this was true. Parker says, "Much has been made in the press of Elvis' supposed difficulties with drugs. The truth is, Elvis only had a drug problem if you consider all medication, even aspirin and sleeping tablets as drugs.... I think it's important that the record be set straight." (Parker, 119). Ed claims that Elvis had people around him that tried to medicate him to keep him from knowing what they were doing. (Dr. Nick here too.) Both my mother and an elderly aunt, before they died, had to take numerous prescriptions. I think my mother took eighteen pills a day. They kept her alive and prescriptions that Elvis took probably kept him alive also.

If Elvis had died on stage instead of face down in his own bathroom, maybe the stories about him would have been different. Maybe stories about him would have been different also if media personalities did not try to jumpstart their careers based upon fantasies about the causes of the death of Elvis. These fantasies were created and then made public for years after his death. This fueled the growth of fictitious tell-all books about Elvis that made people rich. Billy Smith, Elvis' cousin who lived behind Graceland and traveled with Elvis, defends Elvis and his family from attacks such as Albert

Goldman in his book *Elvis*. "He had a way of writing that made me mad as hell. The book was degrading." (Nash, *Mafia*, 1)

"All the crude jokes and ugly rumors can't change the fact that there never was anyone like him and there never will be another again. Elvis was the most extraordinary ordinary man."

Joe Esposito (Esposito, 257)

"But he never forgot who he was and where he'd come from.... There was no harm in Elvis, but there was an awful lot of love." Joe Esposito (Esposito, 256)

Chapter Three

Elvis was Generous. He Made Dreams Come True

"If I stand still, I am a dead man." Elvis
(Hopkins, 135)

On tour, there were scores of people who Elvis supported financially. Charlie Hodge says that eighty-eight people toured with Elvis. Kathy Westmoreland says that Elvis financially supported 300 people. (Westmoreland, 29) (Hodge,154) There were his back-up groups, the Stamps or Jordanaires, Kathy Westmoreland, Sweet Inspirations, at least five band members, Charlie Hodge, a physician, his father, advance people and body guards, a hair dresser, crew and pilots for his personal jet, crew and pilot for leased jets, sound men, lighting men, back-up singers and musicians, wardrobe men, plus valets (Patsy and Gee Gambill), a road manager, Tom Parker and his assistants (at least seven), and friends. When they arrived at the concert location, local ushers, police, and more had to be employed to protect Elvis.

At home at Graceland, he supported Dee Presley (his father's second wife) and her three children, grandmother Minnie Mae, Aunt Delta, two uncles, Vester and Harold Lloyd, a cousin, Billy Smith and his family, plus Charlie Hodge, Lamar Fike, Gary Pepper a disabled person, a personal singing group who sang with him in private, and others who called Graceland their home. (Parker, 123) And in California there was a female house member who he supported, Pat Parry, and a chimp and mid-career there was Priscilla and Lisa Marie, and many more! Even when he was deathly sick, Elvis said he had a lot of people to support. He could not abandon any of them, so he kept working in spite of knowing that he was dying.

Elvis' dream was to buy a farm or house where he could put all of his relatives to work. He not only wanted to take care of his parents but as many people as he could. The first house he purchased for his parents was in 1956. They soon had to look for another location because the fans kept pestering them. There are stories that they even scooped up their lawn as a keepsake.

After reading so many books written about Elvis by

those who surrounded him, it is apparent that they believed that they were responsible for his success in some way. (Of course, most if not all of these people used professional writers to compose their books. Sometimes the person behind the words gets lost when others write for them.) Book after book rehearse stories about how some sang for him in a pinch, protected him, procured girls for him, drove him, had sex with him, packed his clothing, played games, did stunts, guested in movies with him, and took drugs with him.

In their books they pretend to reveal an intimate and grotesque side of Elvis. It is amazing to me that almost all the books deal with Elvis' penis in one way or another. Was he circumcised? Was he potent or impotent? How often did he do it? How come he did not like to be seen naked? And who was the other guy in the room with Elvis and a woman in Goldman's book? Was it Lamar Fike? The witnesses, as I call them, seem to be able to focus primarily on the things that interest them. Were they into drugs, and women, and women, and women? Were they focused on their own sexual fantasies?

Eventually, those around him discovered that he was not a God and so wanted the world to know that he was a human being, or less than a human being. They betrayed him because he could no longer live up to their imagined expectations. Did they want to annihilate or kill him? So often I wonder if the words they told the writers were real? Or were they conjured up to sell books in order to make up for Elvis dying and leaving them high and dry? After all, they were not in his will. Those who lived with him, in the end, treated him worse than the first critics who called him a sausage. They created a horrid myth with the hopes of destroying his global popularity. Fortunately it did not work.

There is a story about Elvis inviting friends to inaugurate his new jet. He was giving gifts to people and his Aunt Delta Mae stood up and began to denigrate Elvis and his gifts. She even pulled out a gun and that gun would have probably brought the plane down. She was intoxicated. She said, "You ain't no damn friend of his! And, I got a good mind to take the .38 I got in my purse and just shoot you dead!" Then, she looked at another hanger-on and said, "And you ain't worth a shit either, you wall-eyed son-of-a-bitch… All you sons of bitches are here for the same thing. You just want his damn money!" (elvisblog) Elvis wanted to kill her at most and then to throw her out of his house at least, because she was living in his home for free. Later, he came crying to Billy, his cousin, and decided to do nothing. He knew his family was riddled with alcoholism that is why he chose not to drink much alcohol.

One of Elvis' favorite television programs was "The Millionaire." Our family watched the program too. Every week this Asian-looking guy by the name of

Marvin Miller delivered a million dollar check to unsuspecting people. The rest of the program told a story of what happened after they received the money. Elvis became that Million Dollar Man. He gave away automobiles, motorcycles, and trucks. By count, Sean O'Neal says, Elvis purchased 2,000 automobiles, and in one day he bought 11 motorcycles. (O'Neal, 15) "One Christmas he purchased ten Mercedes as presents." And on another afternoon he gave away $100K in cars.

Marvin Miller bringing the check.

If someone was drooling over a car where Elvis was shopping, he bought it for him or her. Dr. Nick, Vernon, Jerry Schilling, Ginger Allen's mother, and Mary Jenkins, Elvis' cook, received new homes bought by

Elvis. Elvis gave to more than fifty charities every year. Some of them included homes for the aged, children's hospitals, boys clubs, homes for girls, Goodwill, community centers, heart associations, cancer centers, and more. For Elvis, giving gifts to complete strangers equaled the high he felt when he performed on stage. (Esposito, 33) John Strausbaugh catalogs pages of donations by Elvis, even as co-founder of the St. Jude Hospital in Memphis. (Strausbaugh, 172-178) You could write an entire book about all of his gifts and donations.

To all of his close male associates, he gave gold necklaces handmade with TCB letters with a bolt of lightning. "Taking Care of Business" was his motto that he had taken from the African-American community. The idea for the bolt of lightning could have come from Marvel comics. Some people who were very close to him received necklaces with a golden TLC, "Tender Loving Care." He also gave gold identification bracelets to all of his friends. (Parker, 84) During one concert in 1975 in Asheville, N.C, he gave out jewelry worth $220K to the audience and his band. (O'Neal, 16) These gifts were tokens of his love. Elvis himself wore a cross and a Jewish chai (to life) around his neck. Strausbaugh claims he had a watch that flashed the two symbols. (88) The lightning bolt also decorated a game room in the basement. See below!

Charlie Hodge believed that, "Elvis would never say anything or do anything to put someone down. He always made everyone feel they were a part of it all. No matter how they dressed." (Hodge, 141) Charlie also believed that Elvis gave away things as a way of entertaining himself. (Hodge, 160) But some look upon his giving in a negative way. They argue that he liked to be in control. But there might be a simpler explanation.

Throughout the New Testament, of which Elvis knew well, there is verse after verse criticizing people who are wealthy. Most early Christians did not come from the upper classes so the literature reflects a negative attitude toward the wealthy. Elvis sings a song, "Bosom of Abraham," that has lyrics such as "Well a rich man lives. He lives so well. Children, when he dies will find a home in hell" in his take three version. ("Bosom of

Abraham, Take 3") How does someone sing a song like this who is wealthy beyond imagination? Perhaps Elvis felt guilty for his riches. He often asked the question, "Why Elvis?" Maybe he gave away so much because he was protecting his own soul? His giving is legendary.

Elvis performed benefit concerts such as the Elvis Presley Youth Foundation, cancer research in Hawaii, as well as tornado victims in Mississippi. He wanted to help everyone who needed it. It was like thanking them for his wealth. Estimates claim he donated at least $20 million to help organizations. (O'Neal, 16) Even when Priscilla divorced him, he gave her everything she wanted and then she came back for more, and he gave her $2 million, plus $8000 a month for herself and $4000 a month for Lisa Marie. She was also given 5% interest in "two of Elvis' publishing companies," and proceeds from the sale of the home in California. He loved her and always wanted to be friends with her. She was family and you never abandon family. (O'Neal, 20)

Elvis made so much money that at some point he would have never had to work again, if he had been a selfish person. One of my neighbors in Kansas City seemed to come into a lot of cash overnight. He bought a $400K Motorhome and a jet and I don't know what else? We had dinner one night with him, and I asked about his recent wealth. I said, "Are you helping anyone else?" He did not know what I was asking? I said, "Are you donating or helping anyone with your extra cash?"

He became angry with me for asking the question. "My money is mine and I am not going to share it with anyone. When everyone has lost his or her money and in need I will be sitting on top of a pile of my money. I am not going to give anyone anything." Sounds a little like Scrooge does it not?

But Elvis gave. And he not only gave physical things, he gave spiritual things. His music uplifted people. He wanted them to be happy. He wanted to make their lives better and if a song would do it, he would sing his heart out for them. From everything I have read about Elvis, it seems to me that he lived to perform. He had a special relationship with his audiences. He wanted them to get up close and personal, even when his life was threatened. It was like he was having an affair with them. Everyone loved him and he loved them back. He kept giving.

And people kept coming to him for a handout to fulfill their hopes and dreams. Read the books. From Dr. Nick, to the Memphis Mafia, to his live-in and occasional lovers, people had their hands out and took from Elvis. They lived like the wealthy but were paid small salaries. Vernon often complained but Elvis let them do what they wanted with his money. Elvis dated many women. Stories are told of lovers spending thousands of dollars of Elvis' money on clothing, begging for houses or cars and more, and Elvis could not say "no" to their pleadings. (Westmoreland, 190)

Charlie Hodge describes it well. "They all came. Old movie stars. Young television actors. People who claimed they were Elvis' distant relatives, Fans from Kansas. Hucksters. Investment Counselors. All of them were dreamers, in all varied forms that they can assume. Each had his own private dream. Each saw Elvis Presley as the person who could make the dreams come true." (Hodge, 62) When you read stories of his generosity, you wonder if people gave anything back to him. Charlie Hodge says that he gave a lot to Elvis. He believed he gave up his career to support and coach Elvis.

"Then like a burst of warm sunshine, there was Elvis Presley!"

> May Mann (Mann, 3)

"All the crude jokes and ugly rumors can't change the fact that there never was anyone like him and there never will be another again. Elvis was the most extraordinary ordinary man."

> Joe Esposito (Esposito, 257)

Chapter Four

Elvis loved his Family

"Elvis was a savior to his family."

While Elvis was non-traditional and lived on the edge in many ways, when it came to his parents he was very traditional in almost a biblical way. There are lots of verses in the New Testament that set up a hierarchy in the family with the male at the top and females as servants or subject to the males. These beliefs are foundational within many religious groups who follow the bible.

Elvis listened to his mom and dad and followed their suggestions, even in his early filming career. They traveled with him and hovered over him, and he allowed it. In much the same way, Elvis believed in a traditional relationship with a wife and a manager. While he questioned and almost hated the decisions made by his manager, Tom Parker, he allowed him to dominate him and treat him like a piece of property. (Goldman, 214)

Following in that same type of paternalism, Elvis believed that a woman should stay at home and support her man. She should not have a career. And when he fell in love with Ann-Margret in "Viva Las Vegas," he made a decision that probably hurt him for the rest of his life. No one knows what was said between them but most people think that he demanded that she give up her career, but she could not do it. So they parted but always remained friends.

In interviews with Ann later in life, she always begins to tear when she talks of Elvis. Larry Geller quotes Elvis as saying, "Two egos, two careers--it didn't seem like a lasting thing. Women should be at home to raise a family. That's how I was raised. It's the only way to go." (Geller, 80) Elvis forgot how hard his mother had to work when he was a child and that she often took jobs just so that the family could buy food. Maybe, his ideal was for a woman to stay at home. During the early part of the twentieth century, most males wanted their wives to stay at home. Some considered it embarrassing for a wife to work. My father said the same thing. But when my mother went to work, after my little brother started school, our lives improved. We bought new furniture and added a laundry room and screened-in porch onto the house. Without her salary we would have lived without many necessities and extra space.

Almost every book that has been written about Elvis includes stories about Gladys. She was the center of Elvis' life before he won so much fame. It was Gladys who bore both Jesse, his deceased twin bother, and Elvis. Jesse died at birth and the family claims he would have lived if they had had enough money to go to a hospital. But poverty can kill, especially females. My father's first wife died in childbirth. According to stories, the doctor wept and wept because he could not help her. She bled to death. My grandfather, Joe Gilreath's first wife (or love), died in childbirth with her child. My uncle Homer's first wife died in childbirth. And my own mother had a heart attack at the point of delivering me. She recovered because she was in a hospital, but it was that heart that finally failed her.

It was Gladys who took him to the Church of God, an integrated church, and taught him to sing. Later, when Elvis was a little older, the three of them became a trio. Elvis, Gladys, and Vernon sang at "church parties, revivals, and conventions." (Mann, 13) Vernon played the banjo and later Elvis took up the guitar. They seemed to be quite popular, and although Elvis says that they did not think of getting paid, it is the custom in most places to take up a collection for people who are guests.

Gladys also danced for the Lord in what was called "Buck Dancing." Some sources suggest that Gladys sounded just like Elvis when she sang. Shaking, singing, and dancing were an integral part of worship for Elvis, although his cousin Billy denies that happened in the church. In many churches the dancing, fainting, and speaking in tongues, is believed to be involuntary and a sign that the Holy Spirit has entered someone's life.

Gladys was a firecracker that could explode at any minute. Stories abound of her throwing things at Vernon or others, such as a pot of hot beans or an iron skillet. Although no one speaks of her drinking excessively in her early years, most sources suggest that she was an alcoholic who was also addicted to amphetamines. According to Alanna Nash, all sorts of psychological problems plagued her childhood, and at one point, they left her unable to walk. Lamar Fike said, "Everybody in that family was scared of Gladys and her temper." (Nash, *Baby*, 4) But, again, Billy, a very close cousin of Elvis, only remembers loving stories about her.

Gladys may have had phobias, but she was also a

passionate woman. When she was very young, she left home with a man who was apparently married. It must have broken her spirit and her heart when she discovered his wife. Yet, like Elvis, her dreams kept her going. She wanted to be a grand singer and screen star, but she never really planned that career for herself.

It was Gladys who held Elvis close when his father was away. Many books hype the theory that Elvis and Gladys had this very sexual (sensual) and personal relationship. Gladys was overprotective of him, and that is why he had such an androgynous personality. Elvis was not effeminate, but he chose clothing that most burley men would avoid.

Farley Guy, a friend from high school, remembers that he was a loud dresser, slicked his hair back, and people didn't like him because of his looks. (Burke, *Early Years*, 68) Buzzy Forbes grew up with Elvis and says that nothing they say about the timidity of Elvis is true. "I've heard a lot about how protective Mrs. Presley was of Elvis, that he didn't go anywhere or do anything unless she gave her approval. That's just not true." (Burk, *Early Elvis*, 31) Farley also remembers, "Elvis was a scrapper. No one had to take up for him. Elvis stood his own ground. He was no killer, but he had courage and he was quick. I don't remember there being any gang of bullies at Humes [High School]. The only bully I remember there was Red West." (Burk, *Early Elvis*, 68)

It was Gladys who watched out for him and insisted

that he finish high school. She wanted more for her son than traveling from one low-paying job to another. A high school diploma would help him to win a steady job. It was Gladys who allowed Elvis to entertain young girls in his bedroom at night, sources say. It was Gladys who was afraid of Tom Parker when he came knocking at her door to steal away her son. It was Gladys who intuitively knew when Elvis was in trouble and woke up seeing the flames or hospital bed. One of the cars Elvis was driving actually burst into flames. It was Gladys who told Elvis to slow down. It was Gladys who watched her baby boy enter the Army, knowing that she might never see him again.

Elvis loved Gladys. For some writers his love for her was almost pathological because when she died, during basic training at Ft. Hood, his life was never the same. He never seemed to stop grieving for her. Writers claim that he looked for her in the faces of all the women he met. He drew close to him those females that seemed to resemble his mom. From Priscilla to Ginger, he looked for the eyes of his mother. He even saw her eyes in a photo of Madame Blavatsky, a founder of Theosophy.

I don't think this is unusual. My father died when I was twenty-two and for five years I cried myself to sleep every night. Today I am older than he was when he died but throughout my life I could see faint images of him in characters in movies, politicians, and Native American faces. He was half-Cherokee with red skin and black hair when he died. How can you forget a parent that you loved so much? Elvis could not forget his mother either.

I can't imagine what it would be like to be an only child, but Elvis understood that relationship. "Only" children are an anomaly for bigger families. There is a hidden jealousy of the child by other children and even their parents. They would argue that an only child receives too much attention from both adults. There is also a suspicion that there is something wrong with a family who prefers having only one child. An only child becomes the center of attention and many argue that this damages the child mentally and socially. Elvis was not damaged, but he craved attention throughout his life. There were times when he did not want to be alone but there were also times when he loved being alone, away from the demands of performing and his entourage.

Elvis loved his family and talked about them whenever anyone would listen. He adored his grandmother, Minnie Mae or Dodger. He took her with him to Germany and provided a room for her at Graceland until she died. Larry Geller says that his family was at the center of his life. "As the bus sped up the drive and through the famous Music Gates, we saw the entire household standing on the steps of Graceland, waving and smiling, thrilled to have their Elvis safe at home again." (Geller, 62)

Elvis loved his father, Vernon, also in spite of his personal decisions and inability to manage Elvis' finances. Vernon, unlike Elvis, was not motivated to do much of anything. From all sources, he emerges as a sort of lazy individual who could not apply himself to achieve anything. He lost job after job before moving to Memphis in 1948. He was sent to prison for writing a forged check in Mississippi. Orville Bean's check for a pig was changed to reflect a higher number so that Vernon would receive more money for the pig. Orville caught the error and had him arrested. After this stint in prison, he landed a good job driving a truck in Tupelo but it appears, he was also using a company truck to deliver "moonshine."

The times after the recession in the 1930's were difficult for almost everyone in the United States, but Vernon's difficulties continued for decades. At one point he and Gladys had enough money to begin building a home, but they lost that home. They had to live in the poorest sections of Tupelo near Shake Rag. The name of this area is racially charged. My mother used to tell me that in Williamsburg, Kentucky there was a community of people who lived under the highway bridges, under the train tracks high above, near the Cumberland River. It was called Slab-Town. The Cumberland was dangerous and flooded often so the people who lived there risked their property and lives. I never understood that the name Slab-Town was racially charged also until I was an adult. I always thought "slab" had to do with concrete not bacon. Many of our relatives lived under the tracks with those African-Americans.

After moving to Memphis in 1948, Vernon still had a difficult time finding work that would financially support his family. At one point he hurt his back and Gladys and Elvis had to scramble to earn enough money for the rent. Some sources say she attended Stanley Home Parties and I wonder if she sold Stanley Products. This is a good way to make money if you cannot work full-time or need flexibility in your schedule. My mother sold Stanley Products until my younger brother entered kindergarten.

Elvis needed a competent manager of his finances but could not find one within his family. There is evidence that Marty Lacker kept the books. Sometimes Vernon was stingy with Elvis' money and would not give enough of a living allowance to friends who stayed with Elvis, and other times he lost millions of dollars like the time he sold one of Elvis' jets. Soon after the death of Gladys, Vernon followed Elvis to Germany to support him while he was in the Army. There he fell in love with Dee Stanley. Elvis had to pay off her husband to keep the affair quiet, but would not attend their wedding. But later Vernon traveled with Elvis and stood by his side in some interviews.

There are also some indications that Vernon was a womanizer like his father, Jessie (JD) Presley. Vernon was a handsome guy and some report that he had affairs with other women while married to Gladys. Other reports suggested that he hit her in public during arguments. Some successful people might want to run away from such a dysfunctional family but Elvis did not. He needed them as much as they needed him.

"It worked both ways. Elvis did a lot for me too. He made me wonder who I really was, what kind of person was beneath those layers of preconceived notions. Most of all, he gave me the strength to handle my own beliefs, to measure my own talent, to perform and sing with a freedom I had never known. He was always the stabilizing influence in times of crises. He gave me the ecstasy of being myself. He gave me wings and showed me how to fly. I believe those are the greatest gifts a man can ever give to a woman."

        Kathy Westmoreland (Westmoreland, 116)

Chapter Five

Elvis was an Innovator in Music

"My music is country music with fire in it.
I felt I had to burn it up a little."
Elvis (Westmoreland, 248)

"Nothing really affected me until Elvis, "
John Lennon (Hopkins, 144)

Collage of Photos from Sonny's Collection

Listening to Elvis becomes a religious experience for many. His soft southern tones betray an inner emotion that links with the listener. He does not only sing the notes, he embraces them and makes them live. It is not the song that keeps you listening; it is the intensity of the voice that brings the listener into the singer's story. It is an experience that pushes the listener into a transcendent space and time. Elvis knew that he experienced the same thing when he sang and so added the theme song, "Thus Spoke Zarathustra" from "2001. A Space Odyssey" as the opening to his concerts. Zarathustra takes us back in time at least 3,000 years to the dawn of Zoroastrianism. No wonder they called him "the Nation's Only Atomic-Powered Singer." (Nash, *Mafia*, 67)

Some who traveled with him said that he was too emotional, too sensitive, and too unmanly. Elvis did not fit the image of an emotionless John Wayne. He was creative and energetic, the exact opposite of John Wayne, the mechanical man type. (Westmoreland, 221) Yet it was those very delicate qualities that find expression in Elvis' voice. He was tender and fragile like so many of his fans. As you listen to his voice you can feel his pain and struggles in his own life. Sometimes he is shrill, other times he is coaxing, sometimes he is relaxed, and at other times he is very strong. Was he very ill when he sang, I wonder? Songs from many of his movies are difficult to listen to because of the shrillness of his voice. Elvis was bewildered by life even though he had a great talent, and this comes through in some of his tunes. His voice could also be intuitive and compassionate. He believed, like Maharishi Mahesh Yogi, that all of life is vibrating at a certain speed. Tapping into this rhythmic vibration in essence is tapping into the mind of the Infinite.

I believe that Elvis often thought of his concerts as a way of bringing divine goodness to the people. He lived to perform and to feel the love of the audience. He was there to make them happy, that is all! His music was fun, uplifting, and new to his audiences. He meshed together all sorts of rhythms and interpretative moments in his singing. There was never a dull moment. To sing was a divine gesture of love toward all who accompanied him and to all of his audience. Very good singers can hit perfect notes, but they probably could not take their audience to where Elvis took his audiences. The greatness was in that forever-memorable ecstatic moment on stage.

He did not preach, although on occasion he tried his hand at interpreting biblical verses. There was no social agenda like the music and lyrics by Bob Dylan! He reached out to his audience and accepted their gifts. He asked them to be careful during the concert and not to rush the stage. He talked with them and recognized them. And he worked very, very hard at choreographing the concert and arranging when the songs would be sung, how fast, how slow, and how long. He was a perfectionist and after a show would complain about how his performance could have been better. (Parker, 70) He also loved to hug everyone, yet there were times when he was afraid to step on the stage, "Daddy, it takes a lot of nerve to go out there." (Westmoreland, 136)

Kathy Westmoreland agrees, "He mesmerized me with his talent and his showmanship, his blue sparkling eyes, flashing smile and proud self confident stance. Without a touch of arrogance, he spoke right to his audience in a humble and grateful way. It was obvious that the people adored him. In two hours, all my preconceived ideas about that and his talent went right out the window. He was a genius. There was no doubt about it." (Westmoreland, 9-10) Charlie Hodge also commented upon Elvis' energy and dedication, "Keeping up with Elvis on stage was exhausting. He had a driving power that never let up. He moved to the music. He was a person of great dynamism. Working alongside of him took all the energy we had.... Sometimes I felt sure that Elvis' life was going to kill me. At the same time, I also felt quite sure that Elvis Presley would never die. " (Hodge, 165)

Allan Weiss, who viewed Elvis' first screen test, sensed the tremendous well of energy within Elvis. "The transformation was incredible ... electricity bounded off the walls of the soundstage. One felt it as an awesome thing--like an earthquake in progress, only without the implicit threat." For Weiss the change from a shy country boy into "absolute dynamite" on stage was an awesome site. (Guralnick, *Last Train*, 260).

Very few understood the musical genius of Elvis. Steve Sholes, his musical arranger, said, "Elvis has a fine musical ear and a great voice, a much better voice than people really think he has." (Hopkins, 117) He sang all of the time. (Guralnick, *Last Train*, 291)

Peter Guralnick agrees that Elvis "could play anything after hearing it once or twice." (Guralnick, *Last Train*, 77) Scotty Moore, his first guitar accompanist, said, "I'm thirty-one and he is nineteen, and I've been exposed to all kinds of music and lived through the damn depression, and yet he had the most intuitive ability to hear songs without ever having to classify them, or himself, or anyone I've ever known outside of Jerry Lee Lewis and myself. It seemed like he had a photographic memory...." (Guralnick, *Last Train*, 135)

Walking into the converted racquetball court toward the back of Graceland, you open a door to a stunning display of awards and gold records. See the photo below. It was very difficult to compute his accomplishments.

Wall of Gold Records and Awards

According to Rev. James Hamill, one of Elvis' pastors, Elvis grew up in his Memphis church, The First Assembly of God Church, from the age of thirteen. He was never a member, but he attended more often than his parents. This is the very church where Elvis listened to and met the award-winning Blackwood Brothers. They had already received seven Grammys for their gospel songs. It was in this same church that Elvis auditioned for the group and was told by Jimmy Blackwood, "Elvis, why don't you give it up? You can't sing. You will never be able to sing." (Burk, *Early Years*, 118) And while Elvis listened to the music during church services, he never joined the choir. Many nights after Sunday morning services, Elvis and Hamill's son, Jim, would hike over to East Trigg Baptist Church where they joined in singing African-American and black gospel music. (Burk, *Early Years*, 115-117)

Elvis was also told that he couldn't sing by Jim Denny at the Grand Ole Opry in Nashville after his brief audition. Denny told him to go back to driving a truck. Some say Elvis destroyed his guitar and cried all the way back to Memphis. You have to have faith in yourself and hope for the tomorrows when people of such stature strike down your talent. And these would be signs to Elvis that he was hitting on a new trail that the establishment would reject. What else could he do? If he looked back there was poverty and starvation. He had to keep looking ahead to a future that he could not even imagine. Elvis never gave up, through the tears he kept on working harder and harder.

Scotty Moore may have been one of the people who laid a foundation for Elvis' great success. He was there with him from the beginning and backed him on the guitar on hundreds of songs. Scotty says he loved Elvis like a brother and hoped that Elvis's promises of pay would come to him some day. They never did. Their pay did not equal their support of Elvis, according to Scotty. They resigned as Elvis's back-up band once to protest their pay and were brought back, but Scotty maintained until he died that Elvis had promised more.

When Elvis was teetering on the edge of a failing

career, Scotty was invited to support him during the "1968 Comeback Special." The pay was so little that he lost money on the gig. His story is at odds with the well-known generosity of Elvis. You wonder what was behind the lack of pay and respect for Scotty and Bill Black? The answer may be discovered in the possessive nature of Tom Parker.

While playing the guitar did not come naturally to Elvis, playing the piano and accordion did. "But nobody had to teach Elvis how to play the piano. It was entirely self-taught." (Dundy, 109) While Elvis could not read traditional sheet music, he did read an ancient musical system that he studied as a child. Elvis learned how to sing by the Sol-fa System, Buckwheat Notation. (Dundy, 110) "I could always carry a song. I loved music. I had an ear for it, an ear for tone. If anyone flats or sharps a note, even though I can't read music, I feel it. It goes right through me like a knife." (Mann, 13)

Joe Moscheo, one of the Imperials who sang with Elvis, explains shape note notation in his book *The Gospel Side of Elvis*. "Shape notes evolved as a system that could be easily learned in a weekend.... They were called 'shape' notes because the different notes of the scale each had a different shape.... The shape of each note, not the position on the staff, determined the sound of the note." (Mosheo, 18-19) These shapes were placed in hymnals on a musical staff and did not change regardless of the key in which the song was to be sung. And there many other shape note systems like the Sacred Harp that is used by many groups today.

By permission of www.dolmetsch.com/musictheory1.htm

Many people claim that Elvis always wanted to be a gospel quartet singer. From my point of view, it seems as if he did not want to leave his roots. Those songs and experiences of tent and convention singing stay with you for the rest of your life. I attended YFC (Youth for Christ) or VCY (Voice of Christian Youth) sing-alongs at Cobo Hall in Detroit, Michigan when I was in high school. What a sound! Sometimes there were two thousand kids from all over the suburbs and Detroit, singing at the same time. It did not matter what we sang, it was the sound that uplifted you. And it did not matter that your skin might be a different shade.

Some criticized Elvis for stealing black music and destroying the morals of America. Joe Moscheo continues to explain the musical background of Elvis by recounting stories about his knowledge of African-

American music. Sherman Andrus, a black member of the Imperials, thought that Elvis knew more about black gospel music than he did. Elvis would bring up names of people that he did not know. Elvis collected records and many were amazed at the breadth of his collection, "He had everybody's records: the Harmonizing Four, the Golden Gate Quartet, and those by lesser known black gospel groups." (Mosheo, 30)

There was another side of America that did not appreciate black gospel music or anything that came from African Americans. Many so-called religious people attacked Elvis for bringing down the morals of the United States with his music. Check out all the FBI Reports on him. To these detractors he merely said, "I don't see how any type of music can influence people." (*Elvis. Rare Moments with the King Video.*)

In an interview in Charlotte in 1956, Elvis defended himself. "The colored folks been singing it and playing it just like I'm doin' now, man, for more years than I know. They played it like that in the shanties and in their juke joints, and nobody paid it no mind 'til I goosed it up. I got it from them." (Guralnick, *Last Train*, 289) Yes, it was Elvis' music too! Skin color had nothing to do with listening and loving music.

And what about the tunes and lyrics created by African Americans? How many black songwriters did Elvis make rich when he used their materials? Elvis loved the songs created by Otis Blackwell, an African

American song writer and created his own label, "Gladys Music," where he featured other black writers such as Claude Demetrius. He took Chuck Berry's tunes for a ride also. (Black Song Writers)

Otis Blackwell

    Elvis embraced all sorts of people and loved all types of music. Little Richard appreciated his work. "He was an integrator; Elvis was a blessing. They wouldn't let black music through. He opened the door for black music. " (McDowell, *Genuine Elvis*, 72) Elvis did sing popular songs sung by African Americans, but they had been hits before he released them. (Hopkins, 143) Jean Aberbach, one of the people who owned Hill and Range music company said of Elvis, "Elvis was the finest human beings I ever met ... very religious, very loyal, and not bigoted." (Dundy, 186) Mr. Bobo ran the hardware store in Tupelo remembers Elvis. "I'm proud of Elvis.

He made good; he always tried to do right, he loved his neighbors, he loved his playmates in school, he loved his fans--he just loved people, that's all. Elvis, he'd always come back and see his people--always at night. He was never proud." (Dundy, 101-102)

Elvis' musical genius was built upon the foundation of other innovators. One of his favorite singers of country music was Mississippi Slim or Carbel Lee Ausborn. Hailing from Tupelo also, Elvis was great friends with Slims' brother, James. (Doll, 20) He also loved the Blackwood Brothers, Jake Hess of the Statesman, Arthur Crudup, the Louvin Brothers, Eddy Arnold, Hank Williams, Little Richard, and Jerry Lee Lewis.

He also listened to popular singers like Dean Martin and Mario Lanza. And then there is Sister Rosetta Tharpe. Like Elvis she was from Mississippi. She would dance; play the guitar, sing, and then play the piano in one single song. Her gigs were in Pentecostal churches. Rosetta was born 20 years prior to Elvis, but if you listen to her songs, you can hear a choir behind her. She rocked! Elvis used a choir also, except he had the funds to employ both a band and an orchestra plus two groups of back-up singers for some performances. When I saw him perform in 1976 I could not believe how many people were on the stage. There was an awesome vocal presence.

Sister Rosetta Tharpe

Mississippi Slim

Some called Elvis "the white Wynonie." Wynonie Harris was a singer and shouter from Omaha, Nebraska that liked playing up to the audience. He was born twenty years earlier than Elvis but used the word "rock" in his songs with a little bit of sex. According to Lewis Lord, Elvis listened and adapted Wynonie's songs and moves. (Lord, 2) But his mentors were many. He listened to B.B. King, Rufus Thomas, Ruth Brown, and Howlin' Wolf. He absorbed their talent but never copied it.

Wynonie Harris (Wikipedia)

As a child, Elvis lived on the edge, literally less than a half mile away, from a black community in Tupelo. (Hopkins, 17) Near his home was the Sanctified Church, where services were held in a tent. Music from the rocking worshippers sounded like an orchestra and a choir. John Allen Cooke delivered groceries and Elvis would sometimes ride with him and help him on his route. Says Cooke, an African-American, "The Presleys always liked the blacks and were always on our side. " (Dundy, 130)

Marty Lacker, a member of the group that traveled with Elvis, said that Elvis "absolutely loved black gospel."(Nash, *Mafia*, 35) He enjoyed Roy Hamilton, the Ink Spots, Roy Brown, Brook Benton, Arthur Prysock, Jackie Wilson, and Billy Eckstine. In Peter Guralnick's, *Last Train from Memphis*, there is a photograph of a younger Elvis with B.B. King. How ironic to see them today standing together in the Memphis Visitor Center -- bigger than life as they should be.

Elvis Aaron Presley

B. B. King

The music of Elvis was called "race" music, and most "white" radio stations would not play his songs. Jerry Hopkins, one of the first Elvis' biographers, calls it "integrated" music and claims it was hard to find. (Hopkins, 66) This seems so odd to me. As a teenager living outside Detroit, I knew very well that Motown Records often hid the race of the singers with hopes of selling more records. But a few miles away in Roseville, we loved their songs. We, also, watched the singers on The Dick Clark Show and tried to mimic their dancing and gestures.

Elvis' music was so successful that critics enjoyed berating him. Elvis was called "The Hillbilly Cat," "Elvis the Pelvis," "Ole Swivel Hips," "King of the Western Bop," "Lovesick Stag," "The Whiner," "Yowling Boy," and "Cold-War Weapon." (Hopkins, 208, 242). They attempted to cast him as a deviate or pervert. Even Kathy Westmoreland, upon their first meeting, called herself a "musical snob" for the way she demeaned the music of Elvis. (Westmoreland, 7)

Derogatory reviews of Elvis were intended to destroy his genius and creative energies. To the educated elite, he was abnormal or diabolical or on the edge of insanity drowning in a pool of drugs and women. Jack Gould of the *New York Times* wrote the following about Elvis after his debut on the Milton Berle Show in 1956. "Mr. Presley has no discernable singing ability. His specialty is rhythm songs that he renders in an undistinguished whine.... His one specialty is an accented movement of the body ... that has been primarily identified with the repertoire of the blonde bombshells of the burlesque runway." (Hopkins, 126) Elvis was said to be a derivative of the hootchy-kootchy movement and was engaging in an aboriginal mating dance on stage. Those critics lived in a very narrow cultural world, like many writers today. (And had they ever experienced the hootchy-kootch?)

Recently I read an article in the *Wall Street Journal* that started out with a phrase something like this, "The only traveling I have ever done is from the living room to the bathroom because New York City is the best place to live in the world." Now how does this young man know that New York is the best place if he has never visited anywhere else? There are fabulous cities like Sydney, Australia, Tokyo, Rome, Istanbul, Paris, Anchorage, Seattle, and a thousand more, at least. This man's vision was very narrow just like the vision of Elvis' critics.

Today we would say that Elvis' critics were ethno-centered. They believed that they were superior to everyone else. This can happen anywhere. You can work with academics in a university and find that they are so narrow that they cannot tolerate new ideas or approaches to solving problems, teaching, researching -- you name it. This ethnocentrism is an illness and often infects people from the president of a university to the average student. Elvis faced this type of thinking. This type of thinking is a real hindrance to progress in any area and keeps people from recognizing and learning from geniuses. In fact, these types of people harass and punish geniuses for being different that the paltry status quo. Throughout history they have killed people like Savonarola, Sitting Bull, the Salem witches, Anne Hutchinson, and so many more, for being different and challenging the norm.

Critics also assailed Elvis because they could not understand his differences. They belittled him because of his background and association with African-Americans. There was a preferred musical style that could only be honed in the finest schools by the most educated and the wealthy. How could Elvis ever think that he could jump on a stage and be so popular? He didn't have that ticket but he did it anyway.

Times were changing and society was breaking down barriers of race, class, gender, and wealth. The elite had to run for cover because the lower classes were running at them hard and strong after the influx of the military after World War II and the Korean War.

Unintentionally, Elvis captured the intellectual, emotional, and class-warfare through his music. I was struck by Kathy Westmoreland's comment that Elvis could play classical music perfectly even though he had no training or could not read traditional musical notation. I am also struck at his ability to pick up instruments and play them without lessons, like the accordion, although this is not unusual for people who have music bouncing around in their heads. I remember asking a Caribbean band on a cruise ship to play some of the songs they had created. They did not have any and could not write music. They formed their band, listened to music, and then mimicked the music and lyrics.

Kathy Westmoreland, who had also toured with the Metropolitan National Company, reports that the Library of Congress named Elvis in 1980 as "A Vocal Folk Genius." "It is clear to me that Elvis is thus far the greatest 'interpreter' of songs the world has ever known." (Westmoreland, 249) "Nothing can alter the fact that Elvis was a true American folk singer. He absorbed the sounds of a nation of mixed races--blacks out of Africa, whites from Europe--taking jazz, rhythm and blues, gospel inspirationals, western swing, country and western, bluegrass, and songs of all hard working native Americans." "It's natural that the entire world loved his music, people of all races in the world whose ancestors came to America contributed something to it." (Westmoreland, 248)

Kathy herself was profoundly influenced by Elvis' lifestyle and music. But after learning the music and getting to know Elvis she realized that his music was creating something very special for people and for the whole country, maybe even the world. "It awakened within us the realization of ourselves; that we each and everyone are vibratory creations, hearts beating in time with the universe, united together undeniably in the rhythmical, melodic expression called music. " (Westmoreland, 250)

For instance, people who came to hear Elvis did not sit quietly with their hands folded in their laps. None of the Elvis crowd ever fell asleep while the music was playing. Playing to ninety thousand people in the Astrodome in Houston was an otherworldly experience. Stories are told about how it took the music so long to reach the people and then for the people to respond in an arena that it left everyone spacey. It was difficult to perform and respond to the audience. Many of those who toured with Elvis would experience a momentary deafness after the concert.

Search the net with the phrase "Elvis Presley and music therapy." You will discover link after link that discusses his music and how it has a healing effect on people. Of course, other types of music can also help people, but strange as it may seem, Elvis is mentioned many, many times as a source of health for people who have had a trauma or tragedy in their lives. His voice even calms people who are in mental institutions. (Legge)

There was also a competitive side of Elvis. He wanted to be the best and also wanted "to best " other famous singers. For example, Frank Sinatra was one of Elvis' earlier detractors. "His kind of music is deplorable, a rancid smelling aphrodisiac.... It fosters a totally negative and destructive reaction in young people." (Quotes by Elvis) Sinatra finally came around and apologized through his daughter. But Elvis wanted to best him. He took his signature song, "My Way," and sang it better and with more emotion than the old crooner could do.

Elvis inspired progressive types all over the world to create their own "music on the edge." It began during his life and still continues. Marlene Paula wanted Elvis in her life. She sang, "I want to Spend Christmas with Elvis." Evan Gregory and Gillian Welch have their own renditions of "Elvis Presley Blues" from different epochs in our cultural history. Merle Haggard created and sang "From Graceland to the Promised Land," while Paul Simon sang "Graceland." Dan Reed sings of a "Clean Elvis" and Janis Martin bellows out "My Boy Elvis" and other songs.

Jerry Reed followed with the "Tupelo Mississippi Flash." Check out Larry William's song, "Short Fat Fannie" that uses titles of Elvis hits in 1957. Gregory L. Reece in his book, *Elvis Religion*, also highlights how Elvis' life and music influenced films, novels, art, the founding of religious organizations, and a belief that Elvis is still alive, having been reincarnated in "Orion." Even today you can find tribute artists in almost every major city.

Here in Kansas City we have Jeff Bergen who performs as an impersonator once a month to crowds at Knuckleheads.

Jeff Bergen

"[H]is electric presence, his great rhythmic and sexual charge, his gift for comedy and the very appealing good-humored quality he exuded--these are all star qualities...." Elaine Dundy (Dundy 196)

"Once you saw him perform you never forgot him." Ed Parker (Parker, 57)

"The genius of Elvis Presley was in his music, but the magic was in his voice."

Jerry Schilling (Schilling, 141)

Chapter Six

Elvis was an early Adaptor of Technology

[At Graceland] "The first plane you look at is the 'Hound Dog Two,'

Elvis bought this one in September 1975. It is a Lockheed Jet Star...."
Susan Slade

E lvis loved learning and thinking about new ideas and technology. He would have loved the internet, smart phones, wristwatch computers, and the cloud. His homes and cars were outfitted with the latest gadgets.

In the video, "Elvis. Rare Moments with the King," a reporter interviews one of Elvis' Cadillacs as if the

Cadillac is a person. Inside he found a television, a refrigerator, an icemaker, and a record player. How many other people had automobiles like this forty years ago? Below is one of the pink Cadillacs he bought!

Elvis bought a new 1962 Dodge motorhome which he used to drive back and forth from California to Tennessee. He loved to drive it himself. Perhaps this is where he got the idea of turning a Cadillac into something he could almost live in? Or was it riding around in one of those limos? Check out the 1962 Dodge Motorhome earlier in this chapter, courtesy of Chrysler Group LLC." Did Elvis' motorhome look like this before it burned up?

Many want to lay responsibility for Elvis' satellite concert from Hawaii in 1973 in the hands of his manager Tom Parker. I am sure that Tom and his team handled the logistics, but Elvis certainly had a hand in it. Elvis was fascinated by space travel. Television and the movies transported him to another universe, in a way, and he could see transporting himself to people all around the globe. In an interview just before the Hawaii concert, Elvis was humbled by the possibility of reaching so many people at the same time.

Elvis Monopoly from Sonny's Collection

When Elvis was younger he would not fly in an airplane, presumably because his mother was afraid for him to fly? After she was gone, he wanted his own palace in the sky, like Air Force One. He bought a Conair 880 and named it "The Lisa Marie" with a TCB symbol clearly at the back of the airplane. It included a bedroom, conference or eating area, with a seating capacity of 29.

He also leased a smaller aircraft, a Fairchild F-27 and then purchased an Aero Jet Commander. Some of his other purchases included a Gulfstream G-1, a Lockheed Jet Star, and a classic Dessault-Falcon. (Elvis Australia) His father leased the Jet Star but lost hundreds of thousands if not a million dollars in the process. At one point it looked like the lessee had stolen and re-sold the plane. Photo below is from inside the Lisa Marie at Graceland.

Elvis liked gadgets and things made of metal like automobiles, airplanes, golf carts, motorcycles, bumper cars, and more. When the Beatles visited Elvis in California, they were amazed at the clickers he had to the television sets. I wonder if he was a beta tester? Hidden inside a cane he carried with him, later in life, was a knife that could spring out if needed.

He was also interested in the technology that produced sound for his concerts. "Elvis' musical talents also encompassed the inner workings of his sophisticated sound system. The sound system was the best that money could buy." (Parker, 69) He worked with the soundmen on mixing the sounds and the placement of amplifiers. They worked out the best sound during the opening acts and then Elvis would emerge during the second half of the show.

While Elvis appeared to be against traditional education, he loved to study and read. He certainly would have utilized online education. According to Ed Parker, one of his karate teachers and a friend, "I had become aware of Elvis' intelligence and photographic memory as far back as 1960. " (p. 49) Ed believed that Elvis was genius in many, many ways. Not only did Elvis love new technology but he also loved learning about new and classical religions. He absorbed as much of what was "new" and tried to employ it in his own life. In my second book, we will explore the frontiers of new religions where he sent his mind and heart.

Inside of the Lisa Marie

"Elvis was a true original...."

Elaine Dundy (Dundy, 196)

"There is the word icon, and I don't think anybody has topped that ... not one single person has ever topped Elvis,"

David Lynch, Film Director (Nash, *Baby*, xvi)

Chapter Seven

Elvis Lived on the Edge of Traditional Morality

"It was a way of life." Jo Smith (Nash, *Mafia*, 611, 617)

"His world was so unreal. We were like vampires. We only lived at night."

"Elvis liked unusual people." Charlie Hodge (Hodge, 85).

Used by Permission of Igor Yuzov

I asked Igor Yuzov of the "Red Elvises" about the reason that he began his group in the name of Elvis. The Red Elvises are a dance band hailing from Russia/Ukraine that was inspired by Elvis. Igor had a dream that Elvis was telling him to sing rock music. Igor said, "Elvis is one of the most influential performers in the world and probably most imitated too. Everybody loves to make fun of him even Elvis himself. He had a great sense of humor."

And the Red Elvises capture that sense of humor and zest for ecstatic living. Their songs are about sex (love?), drinking, drugs, and rock 'n roll today. Elvis liked playing with people and especially playing with sex. To Patrician Vernon of the New York Times he said, "They all think I am a sex maniac. They're just frustrated old types, anyway. I'm natural." (Hopkins, 153) When Elvis invited a young lady into his room at a hotel, no one really knew what went on. More often than not he would talk to her or read to her from one of the books he was studying. But the world thought there was more going on in there than just reading.

Igor Yuzov. By permission of Igor Yuzov. Selvidge photo.

The myth about Elvis' preoccupation with sex began early. Billy Smith, a cousin of Elvis, told a story about Elvis watching women dancing when he was four or five. He could see under their skirts and yelled out "Oh, my peter." Apparently he had become aroused watching the women carry on in such a wild fashion. (Nash, *Mafia*, 18)

Kathy Westmoreland remembers a quote from Elvis that seems to ring true of the times in the later part of the twentieth century. Elvis said, "Marriage is an outdated institution. It just doesn't work for most people and ought to be abolished." (Westmoreland, 55) During the mid-twentieth century, sexuality and the rules of engagement were changing. People did not want the traditional lives of their parents or grandparents. They wanted something different, so they began to explore different types of relationships. Elvis was probably part of this movement.

Lamar Fike claims that Elvis never wanted to be married. He asked a lot of women to marry him but he never wanted to be married. (Nash, *Mafia*, 76) "If Elvis had jumped as many girls as it was rumored, he would have had blood running out of his nose all the time. He would have weighed thirty pounds. He'd have been nothing but hair, teeth, and eyes." (Nash, *Mafia*, 163) Marty Lacker says that Elvis also told him that he did not want to be married. When he finally agreed to be married, it was not his idea. (Nash, *Mafia*, 393)

Certainly Elvis inherited the love of women from his father. Vernon loved the women as much as Elvis did, (as we have indicated earlier) and fidelity was not at the top of his list. I remember reading a best-selling book in the 1970's entitled *Open Marriage* by Nena O'Neill and George O'Neill. Feminist in nature, it advocated friendship with the opposite sexes outside of marriage and multiple sexual partners within marriage. Of course, this was what was actually happening all over the United States as people were experimenting with different types of relationships.

Experimentation within and outside of traditional marriage is not new. The Shakers tried celibacy and many utopian communities, such as The Oneida Community, experimented with multiple marriages and multiple sexual liaisons. The Counter Culture movement of the 1970's also experimented with all types of living and sexual relationships.

It was a reaction to the rigid puritanical views of older generations. Elvis just made it public, even though people had been doing it since sex was discovered. Young people did not want to fit themselves into neat little boxes. They did not want females to be punished socially for having a child outside of marriage. Women wanted to be free to live alone or with others. They did not want to be cloistered behind fathers or family walls. They wanted freedom to find different lifestyles and relationships. The seeds for "Gay and Lesbian" rights were certainly born during these times. These young people were doing "it" out in the fields and in every way and place possible.

Elvis was no more flawed or less flawed than this generation. But he was more honest about the kind of lifestyle he wanted to live than most people. And to be truthful, any type of relationship (like marriage) that proves lethal to growth and change should be abandoned. Since the time of Elvis, traditional marriage is still a majority choice for most people. Says Westmoreland (182) "He was simply not good husband material and not a man you could depend on to watch over you and share your good times and your bad times."

Elvis had a magnetism about him. I often wonder if people like Elvis have an over abundance of hormones. And do those hormones travel over distances to other people? Studies have shown that hormones in the sweat glands of female athletes can hop over to males. Both men and women were attracted to Elvis. For example, the Memphis Mafia (the gang that hung around him) claim they loved the man. Lamar Fike calls those whom he gathered around him "misfits." And Billy Smith called himself and others "outcasts." (Nash, *Mafia* 104, 208) He chose people who were "underdogs" and then tried to help them. But this resulted in a dependency upon Elvis. They waited for and craved attention from him. They wanted to be around him not only for the perks that Elvis brought to them but because Elvis meant so much to them.

Nick Adams was an early friend of Elvis. Some argue that he was a plant by Tom Parker his manager. Nick was to keep Elvis in line. Others assert that Elvis had a sexual relationship with Nick. He may or may not have? After Elvis' marriage in 1967, Nick ended up dead in his hotel room in 1968, apparently an overdose.

Some reports suggest that Elvis paid Nick's bills as he did for many. We do know that Elvis fervently denied that he was gay or bisexual in any way. We must remember that to be "openly" gay during this time in our history might have destroyed an entertainer's career. Did they not have to sign a morality clause in contracts? And

Elvis came from a very traditional Christian background that would have called such activity a "sin." If he was gay, he hid it to protect himself. No one knew that Johnny Mathis, Rock Hudson, Sal Mineo, Raymond Burr, Paul Winfield, Richard Chamberlain, and so many more entertainers were gay until almost the end of their careers.

Both Lamar Fike and Billy Smith say they were "married" to Elvis. He was the center of their lives even while they were married. "I was married to Elvis. Hell, we all were. There was never any question where my allegiance was. My wife was secondary. And most of the guys felt that way.... The Catholic Church would hope to God it has monks and nuns as dedicated as we were. " (Nash, *Mafia*, 270)

Kathy and several of the Memphis Mafia say that Elvis was not as promiscuous as the tabloids described him. He did not engage in harmful sexual practices. He liked women and wanted to get to know them. He liked meeting new people, and this was his way of meeting the world. He could not go to a party or travel to a distant land with a new group of people. He was too famous and too vulnerable. When the doors closed to his hotel suite, the writers could only fantasize about the activities, and many books about Elvis are filled with fantasy.

But Elvis did fall in love a lot! One of the quotes

about Elvis' choice of women is comical. After his stint in the Army, Elvis "returns with an underage concubine, army brat Priscilla Beaulieu, closing a bizarre deal with her parents which she becomes his live-in girlfriend at Graceland...." (Strausbaugh, 77) But that little agreement eventually made Priscilla and Lisa Marie wealthy beyond anyone's imagination. While in Germany, Elvis also fell in love with other women. Many stories are told about Elisabeth Stefaniak, who he later hired to manage his fan mail. Some stories suggest that she slept with him every night to keep him company. (Hodge, 36)

Was Elvis linked with the mob? The fifties were filled with Eisenhower, McCarthyism, and the Mafia. Dundy hints that the Mafia wanted to move into Elvis' career because it was so lucrative. (Dundy, 189, 250) They wanted to buy a percentage. There is evidence that the Mafia controlled Casinos in Las Vegas and elsewhere. Tom Parker claims that he did not sell part of Elvis' contract, but you have to wonder that maybe he did involve himself with organized crime? And that entry came down on Elvis' head and life.

There are all sorts of other hints and reports that organized crime dogged Elvis. He feared whoever was threatening him. "Larry, [said Elvis], this is a dangerous universe,"...No matter who you are, the higher you are, the more dangerous it is...." (Geller, 183) Elvis kept on talking about how people used to dump bodies in the river. Now those same people appear to be legitimate businessmen. They talk to you but they can be lethal.

Jerry Hopkins writes about what an odd bird Tom Parker was, probably psychotic. Among his earlier carney jobs was palm reading. Palm readers exercise a lot of control over the person they are touching. "On all sides [Elvis] was surrounded by super-salesmen and easily exploitable freaks. The sword swallower was one of the few in the world who swallowed fluorescent light bulbs and then turned them on so you could see his chest glow, geeks bit heads off live chickens, the tattooed lady invited you to examine almost all of her body, midgets ran between the barker's legs, and dozens of fast-talking con-men invited thousands of passers-by to step right up and pitch pennies, throw baseballs, shoot rifles, have their fortunes told, watch kootch dancers and buy canaries, lemonade and foot-long hot dogs." (Hopkins, 84) Tom, while traveling throughout the country, even sold some type of medicinal remedy called "Hadacol" but denied it later in life probably because of the investigations and lawsuits.

Tom Parker

Andreas Cornelius ("Dries") van Kuijk,

Elvis' morality reaches beyond what someone does with the lower parts of their bodies. More than anything in his life Elvis linked both light and dark-skinned people together. His heritage included Native American and Jewish blood. Larry Geller says that his Aunt Martha Tackett Mansell was Jewish. I have always wondered about his grandmother Rosella Presley, called a freethinker by Alanna Nash, who brought ten children into the world without identifying their fathers. Some say that she slept with someone who had Cherokee blood, (Nash, *Baby*, 9) but I wonder if she had African-American suitors. Some of Elvis' early pictures, before his surgeries, seem to reflect African-American physical characteristics. (Or, perhaps those features were a result of his father smashing him against the wall in his sleep one night.)

As a child growing up outside Detroit, racism was the name of the game in my parent's generation. I hated the bigotry and slanderous language used toward people of color by adults. The races were to be kept separate. My father did not recognize, as a half-Cherokee, that he was also a person of color. And his ancestors faced discrimination in much the same way as African-Americans when I was a child.

Traveling south to Nashville, Knoxville, and southern Kentucky with relatives, dark-skinned people sat outside the courthouses as we drove through sleepy towns. They looked like they did not have anything to do. Later I realized that it was cooler under the trees and they did not have air-conditioned homes, if they had homes at all. Culture shock hit me when we stopped with my aunt and uncle at a restaurant one summer somewhere in Tennessee. Dark-skinned men wearing white gloves served us. It was very odd and I did not like the divisions I saw.

Taking a job in North Carolina, probably twenty years later, I worked for a retail company that still had two fountains, one for whites and one for blacks. I was instructed to use only the restroom that was marked "White Women." There were no African-Americans working as salespeople at this retail store. Some African-Americans worked in shipping where no one could see them. And sales people told me that they did not allow dark-skinned people to try on shoes in the store because the white people would not buy them if they did. Blacks had to go around to the service area to try on shoes.

When teaching at a small women's college in South Carolina, dark-skinned people served all light-skinned people wearing little black outfits with white aprons and white gloves. It was too much for me; I never went to another college social. Today in Missouri, often if you go to a restaurant, African-Americans are doing the cooking not the serving, even when they own the restaurant.

And while we may claim that the racial divide has

been closed, it is not gone. We could talk about the small number of dark-skinned people in Higher Education and education in general. In fact we could discuss why so many inner cities today are filled with poor dark-skinned people, often on the edge of crime. This is a huge societal problem that cannot be discussed here. But Elvis understood the prejudice, not only against blacks, but also against poor white people in general. His life was a beacon to both of these groups, to which many of us belonged, as they held hands demanding change that would make their lives more bearable.

Elvis also challenged the traditional role of "white masculinity" (Nash, *Baby*, xv). In his first movie, "Love me Tender," he plays the brother of Richard Egan who had been away fighting in the Civil War. When Eagan returns, he discovers that his best gal has married Elvis. Egan is taller, apparently stronger, and a physically fit man-of-his-day. He was something to swoon over. But the moviegoers swooned over Elvis, the young somewhat effeminate man with the soft skin and big eyes. Egan did not understand it, after all he kept himself fit and ready for action. Elvis wins the girl and keeps the girl until the end!

According to Erika Doss, a woman who has studied Elvis culture extensively, in society "male pleasure has traditionally been dominate." (Doss, *Power*, 7) Elvis' personality, style, and love of women challenged that domination. Elvis did not want to dominate. He wanted to love and make females happy. He did not want his audience to serve him in a particular way. Perhaps the females in the audience screamed because they had found someone who did not want to dominate them in a way where they would lose themselves, as any slave does. Elvis' attitude toward women in the audience was one of equality. He treated them as if they were superior. Traditional white males watched the women and then looked at themselves and their relationships with females. Those relationships were paltry compared to what Elvis offered and it made them feel small. It wasn't Elvis they hated; they hated themselves for not being Elvis. The hate they streamed toward Elvis was misdirected.

This image of Elvis challenged manly men into wondering about what really made a man attractive to females. If a guy like Elvis could get all the girls then there would be nothing left for them. It is no wonder that men screamed all over the country that Elvis was "recognized as a threat to mainstream U.S. culture." (Nash, *Baby*, xiii) In a way, he was eroding the confidence of every traditional white male. And, just maybe, they couldn't even move their hips.

And let's just think about that "race" voice that belonged to Elvis. In some states during the nineteenth century if a black man had sex with a white female, even consensual, it could be grounds for a hanging. (Selvidge,

See chapter on "Free Blacks" in *Life Everlasting*, to be published.) So Elvis was eroding the white traditional male authority on two grounds. They were so afraid of him that they struck back at every opportunity.

Sex roles were changing in society. Since WWII and the Korean War females had worked side-by-side with men in the factories. They weren't down on the farm hooked up to oxen. They knew they could take care of themselves economically and so they weren't looking for the cave-man type husband that would hover over and smother them at home. They were finding new freedoms and Elvis just happened to be one of those freedoms.

Even today males often do not "love" females. They are told that they should marry and that they should take care of a family. And many males want to place their last name on progeny. But do they love being with females? Do they love to do the things that females do? Are they tender and caring and do they help to take care of the children and the home? Many men do, but many don't. Females become a sort of star on the foreheads of the males. Look who I have bedded? Look who I have married? It is an ego trip. Females are to be used not cherished.

After marriage, the males resume their boy's games and outings and leave the females to manage everything that resembles domicile life. For social outings and meetings at work, they prefer the company of males. But

Elvis was different, "He loved being with girls. (Yet, he chose to hire primarily males to take of him.) Later on, I found out whether the girls were eight years old or eighteen or sixty five or seventy, he just liked women," says Alfred Wertheimer, an early photographer of Elvis. (Nash, *Baby*, xiv)

"You! You, who loved him. You, who bought his records, attended his concerts, and saw his movies. You who stood in line for hours to batch a glimpse of him. You were the siren of his life. You held his future in your fickle fingers, and he feared the loss of your love more than the loss of his own life." Ed Parker (Parker, 165)

Chapter Eight

Elvis Trusted People

"I was privileged to share his most private moments, I witnessed his unequal generosity, watched him give of himself to everyone. We are all just a little bit better for his having been here."
Charlie Hodge (*The Elvis I Knew*)

Sonny's Collection

Elvis trusted the Memphis Mafia, his parents, Priscilla, and his managers. In order to have any sort of stable life we have to trust people, to trust that they are doing what they are supposed to do. We have to trust that they are who they say they are. In many respects, Elvis was naive because of that trust. He wanted to think that people were capable, trustworthy, honest, and had his best interests at heart. Sometimes, even though people might think they are doing their best, they are actually harming another person.

Elvis had only a high school education and was a humble and even contrite person. He had very little of the arrogance that Tom Parker possessed. Vernon and Gladys, had even less of an education than Elvis with no experience in the music industry. Gladys feared Tom, but she was won over to sign the contract after a meeting with Hank Snow.

For the edge upon which Elvis teetered as an entertainer, his every day life was much more complicated. He respected authority as we have discussed. After all, the Bible teaches you to respect your parents and to love your neighbors. But Elvis respected Tom Parker too much. He respected him so much that Elvis became what many have called his "dancing chicken." George Klein makes the same observation in his book, *Elvis: My Best Man*, "[Tom Parker] was lucky enough to be working with one of the greatest talents of the twentieth century, and, in too many ways, he treated that talent just like another dancing chicken." (Klein, 156)

Tom Parker even used the analogy himself of

dancing chickens. Before big events he scheduled in the south, he would bring a hot plate and two chickens to sit outside an arena. Most municipalities in the south charged a tax on people who were attending an event other than one that was agricultural. So to avoid the tax, Parker would hook up the hotplate and tie the chickens so their feet were on the hotplate. They danced and so, he could then call the event agricultural. Today he would be jailed and fined for animal abuse. Elvis was the dancing chicken for Parker. Tom worked Elvis to death.

When I first began researching Tom, I kept imagining Elvis to be a dancing monkey. Old films portray a guy sitting on a corner while playing an accordion with a rope around a dancing monkey's neck.

There are several stories told by Tom Parker that reveal his attitude toward Elvis and to other human beings. He used to take care of the elephants when he was employed at a circus. He explained that when the elephants are young, a rope is placed around their necks to control and direct them. When they mature and become so huge that they could easily break away, they do not. The noose around their necks still controls them. The chicken or the elephant had been so socialized into subservience that he could not separate from Parker.

And when Elvis tried to leave Parker, he demanded $10 million to cancel the contract, ten million that Elvis did not have. So the rope never left his neck. But you always wonder why he did not go to an attorney to try and work out a deal?

Stories are told of Parker commandeering Elvis after a fall in the bathroom and firing some of the staff who supported him. Or, forcing Elvis to perform at a concert after Dr. Nick revived him by forcing his head into an ice bucket. At other times Elvis seemed to be in a stupor and went along with everything Parker wanted, even if he was totally against it. Several tell stories about Parker hypnotizing members of the Memphis Mafia. Could he have also mesmerized Elvis and kept him under hypnotic control?

Elvis wanted challenging roles in films. Tom Parker wanted money. Elvis did not want to sing in films, but Parker said that if he did not sing, there would be no money. Elvis wanted to do concerts while he made films. Parker would not allow it. Elvis had an opportunity to entertain the troops when he was in the Army, and Parker forbade it. Elvis wanted to tour Europe and the Far East. Parker would not arrange the tour. Elvis was offered the lead role in *A Star Is Born* with Barbra Streisand, and Parker blocked it. His kid wanted more money for the work and top billing. The film and album for *A Star Is Born* were huge successes and re-released on Blue Ray in 2013.

Elvis needed to rest from his two shows a night while in Las Vegas but Parker kept booking him, as if he were an animal. Even when the shows sold out while on tour, Tom Parker would add a matinee. Elvis could not do two excellent shows a day. He said, "I feel bad doing two shows a day, Ed, hell, I'm not even awake during the first show, and I have to be ready for the next. When I'm finally awake, I'm too tired by then to do the second show. I hate doing two shows a night. I can't do a good job doing both. One show a day is all I want to do. I'm going to have to stop these matinee shows. They're killing me." (Parker 96)

Tom Parker used the title of "Colonel" which he did not earn, and loved the word "exploitation" and employing it. I think he took the title because the military dishonorably discharged him. It was like saying, "So what! I don't need you to recognize and promote me, I can make up a title for myself or bribe someone to give it to me." After reading numerous books about him including Alanna Nash's, *The Colonel*, I have concluded that the man was a psychopath. (I am not a therapist but the term seems to fit.) He enjoyed dominating those who threatened his ego. Meetings were often held in the men's restroom, with Tom sitting on a toilet. Elvis was an easy mark. Tom stalked his talent, stealing Elvis away from several other interested parties, and then finally winning a contract to manage him.

Elvis wanted to tour the world and Parker turned

down multi-million dollar offers in other countries. There was one for a million dollars for a single concert in the U.K. and another multi-million dollar offer for a tour in Japan. (O'Neal, 68) I have often wondered why Tom Parker allowed Elvis to go into the Army. He could have obtained an exemption for being an only child or any number of reasons. Parked claimed that to steal Elvis away from the public would make Elvis "hotter." If they can't see him, they will want more of him and buy more albums and records. This strategy worked and Elvis had multiple number one records on the charts when he returned home from Germany.

Watching the video, "Elvis. Rare Moments with the King," for a second time, I heard these words from Elvis, "Just before I went into the Army, we were planning a tour of Europe." Parker was never going to take Elvis abroad. But he did allow Elvis to experience travel in the military. I wonder if he arranged for "his boy" to go to Germany, a very safe place in 1958. Could this be the kindest thing that Parker ever did for Elvis?

Of course Parker could not travel outside the United States because he did not have a passport nor could he obtain one because he was not a citizen of the United States. No one understood the reasoning at the time. Later, it was discovered that Parker was living under an assumed name. It is alleged that he had fled the Netherlands bound for the USA after brutally murdering a woman when he was young. He left his home and never communicated with his mother or the rest of the family until he was discovered late in life. In his early years in the United States, he falsified papers, saying he was an orphan, to gain entrance into the United States Army. After signing up for another tour of duty, Parker went AWOL. No one knows why this happened. Returning to his base, he was punished and placed in confinement for a couple of months. Parker experienced a total psychological breakdown. He was taken to a mental hospital and later released from the military. He never reached the level of Colonel. But he ordered Elvis around as if he really was a Colonel and Elvis was a private.

For almost ten years Parker scheduled two or three no-content "B" motion pictures per year for Elvis. Finally in 1968, after Elvis was almost a has-been, his "1968 Comeback Special" launched his singing career again. This is the special where he sang, "If I can Dream" at the end of the program.

The song made a statement about African-American struggles but it was also Elvis' struggle too. He was in prison. Elvis was strong enough to argue with Parker about the inclusion of the song in the special instead of a Christmas carol. This may have been a first and only independent moment for him. Steve Binder, a guiding force in his strength, remembers, "That strange hypnotic way he had of exercising total control and power over Elvis. That kind of hold is totally unexplained in terms either of deals or loyalties between people. " (Dundy, 202)

Steve challenged Elvis to think for himself, to follow his creative instinct. It was a real struggle for Elvis. Choosing to go against the old man was frightening. He chose to sing a tune at the end of the "1968 Comeback Special" that was written specifically for him and based upon Martin Luther King's "I have a Dream" speech. As Elvis rehearsed and sang "If I Can Dream" many times, the last and most successful time he lay curled up in a fetal position in the dark. But, all the same, he did it. Some like to identify this time in his life as a resurrection. His career had virtually died and with the help of a creative staff and Elvis' enormous talent, the career began to soar. He entertained to mostly sold-out crowds for the rest of his life. His concerts number almost 1400 (numbers vary) as he crisscrossed the United States.

Parker jumped off the cliff (not literally) after the 1968 special and scheduled the band, singers, and Elvis to perform on a daily basis. The tours were excruciating and debilitating. As we have suggested previously, Elvis developed physical problems with his colon, his back, his eyes, his heart, diabetes, and high blood pressure. Cortisone shots for pain made him swell. Many of those illnesses could be traced back to poor nutrition and illness when he was young. Elvis often had pneumonia or close to it and was rarely treated at a hospital. You wonder if his illnesses were related to his heart. If you look at Elvis' physique when he first started touring in his teens, he was very thin, too thin and almost underdeveloped. Larry Geller visited Tupelo one day with Elvis. It was not until years later did he begin to understand the devastating effects of malnutrition and poverty on Elvis. Geller felt "naive" with regard to this kind of poverty. (Geller, 74)

Tom Parker cared little for the man with a rope around his neck. He singularly cared about the cash that was flowing into his pockets. Parker often took money up front in cash and no one really knows what happened to that money.

He set up companies and sold Elvis paraphernalia, including signed autographs of Elvis. He wrote contracts that paid him more money than Elvis on everything that Elvis created and every performance. According to Sean O'Neal, "There is evidence that both Colonel Parker and RCA are guilty of collusion, conspiracy, fraud, misrepresentations, bad faith, and over reaching." The deal to sell Elvis' recordings, "may have been valid on their face, but they were unethical, fraudulently obtained, and against industry standards." (O'Neal, 69).

Parker became addicted to gambling. Some say that he could lose a million dollars a night. Sources said that he owed $30 million to the Las Vegas Casinos, particularly the Hilton. When Parker died, after earning more than $100 million, his estate was worth less than a million. Many people think that Elvis often worked for nothing just to pay off Parker's debts.

Perhaps selling Elvis' canon of tunes to RCA was a way to pay off Parker's debts and to repay the Mafia? Men in dark suits visited Elvis, and sources suggest that organized crime threatened him, and told him to keep performing or else his ex-wife and child would be hurt. I wonder if Parker created many of those threats just to control Elvis? There is evidence that he did this in Mexico. Not many of the perpetrators of the threats were found. One of Elvis' responses was to cocoon himself, like a caged animal.

According to Ed Parker, "Elvis was a target for everyone with a need or a scheme.... Threats to his life were commonplace. The threats were genuine. You don't remember hearing of these threats for good reason. Every threat had to be shielded from the press and hidden from the public. That was the policy.... Any deviation could have cost Elvis his life." (Parker, 92) Take a look at some of the FBI files on Elvis. Letters came to the FBI claiming that Elvis was killed in an airplane crash. Threats of kidnapping and killing were a regular occurrence. And local police often gave protection to Priscilla and Lisa Marie.

Ed Parker remembers threats of assassinations where people demanded $60K in cash. Terrorists claimed that they were going to kill Elvis in order to control other performers. They said that a bomb would be placed in one of the gifts that were thrown on stage for Elvis. One day while writing autographs for his fans, a young man off to the side of him, took out a knife and laid it on his wrist. Without looking at the man, Elvis diffused the situation by threatening the man. The man closed the knife and walked away. (Parker, 95)

Tom Parker rarely showed emotion toward Elvis and did not try to help him with personal issues. Perhaps he was jealous of him. Elvis was everything he could never be. He was an American, handsome, talented, thin, kind, generous, lacking ego, and the women flocked to him. Parker controlled him when it came to anything that influenced his cut of the money Elvis was earning. Many think he forced Elvis to marry Priscilla because he was afraid that a story would surface that Elvis had sex with an underage child. Perhaps she was pregnant. The fallout could have ruined his career.

Lacking a formal education or skills, Parker gravitated, always, to the circus where dropouts found a place to live and work. He began as a carney and worked his way up to hawking country singers. When Elvis died, he showed no emotion. Some say that he even wore a party shirt and hat to the wake. But he did make a remark that only the body was dead, "Elvis lives," which meant that he could still exploit his talent and his name even after he was dead. "The true master of exploitation was waiting in the wings. He had been preparing for Elvis' death for some time. You might even say he had prepared for that moment since they first met in 1955." (O'Neal, 45)

Elvis' himself could never intentionally harm anyone, even though he was known to shoot out a television set or throw things in a burst of frustration, as his mother did. He trusted that others were like him. He believed in the natural goodness of people. He was obviously wrong.

"It was Elvis whose name penetrated artificial political boundaries. It was Elvis who gave a beautiful sense of love, and peace, and understanding, and sharing and caring between us all in the Elvis World...."

"No matter, however, how high he climbed, he never forgot his Humes Years or the real friends he made there." Bill Burk (*Chronicle*, 4 and *Early Years*, 132)

Chapter Nine

Elvis was a Southerner

"I'll tell you one thing. I sometimes get lonely as hell. " Elvis
(Dundy, 284)

Photo of Sam Cox, Elvis, and Marion Keisker that is on the wall at Sun Records. Taken in 2013 at Sun Records

We learn, if we are to survive in our jobs or within a family, sometimes we have to isolate ourselves. People don't always have our best interests in their plans. There are those who envy any kind of success and prey upon us or indict us without cause or evidence in order to harass us. Our pressure is small compared to what Elvis experienced. He had the world knocking at his door.

Early on, he learned that he was not one of them. He was not educated in the finest of acting schools in the north. He did not come from a wealthy and powerful family. His speech was different. His mannerisms were different. He dressed differently and ate very different foods. His morals were different. His social skills were different. In some of the books about Elvis, stories are told about how young actresses were cruel to him before he became a world phenomenon. Did they call him a "hick" or a "hillbilly?" Did they not stay away from him because he was so different? After he became the highest paid actor in Hollywood, they came to pay homage to him. But in the early years it was different.

While some of the songs in "Jailhouse Rock" were fabulous, it is difficult to listen to the dialogue that was assigned to Elvis. Elaine Dundy in *Gladys and Elvis* claims that he did not show up at the movie's opening in Memphis because he hated it so much. The writers and producers had taken his own life and twisted it into a story that he detested. They told a story that belittled him and his family with hints of homosexuality. (They were so jealous of him!) No wonder he began to build walls around himself!

We wonder what it was like for Elvis to transition from Tupelo/Memphis to Hollywood? It may have seemed like traveling to the moon or outer space.

Having visited numerous countries, I know that there is a cultural shock that can happen to you. You don't even know that you are experiencing it until later. You feel as if you cannot move. I remember getting off a train the first time I visited Tokyo after flying for what seemed to be twenty-four hours. I walked up the steps and stood on the street corner. There were thousands of people going home after work, and they were standing on the opposite corner. I looked at them and I could not move. They began crossing the street. I kept thinking, "Where will I walk?" I needed more space around me. I could not be touched or shoved by all of those people! I finally made it across the street and began looking for a place to eat. I could not eat or drink.

On another trip, I had no problems walking throughout Tokyo by myself. None of the people threatened me. No wonder Elvis brought his family with him to Germany, Hollywood, and when he was touring. He needed some normal moments in his life.

How did Elvis adjust to a totally different culture? Yes, he had been to New York but Steve Allen had made fun of him on television as he sang "Hound Dog" to a canine. He did not understand that he was the brunt of the joke. (Steve Allen says he understood the gig.) Tom Parker would throw a stuffed dog on stage while Elvis was performing. It was humiliating. He played up to it but hated it. He also played a dumbed-down cowboy in a silly western sketch that made him look stupid on the Steve Allen show. Yes, he had sung on the Ed Sullivan Show but they banned his dancing moves. He was too lewd. (Some sources say that it was Parker who suggested the close-ups that left out his moves.) Larry Geller, his hairdresser, recalls that Elvis said, "Man, all I did is what came natural! I guess if you have a dirty ol' mind, that's exactly what you're gonna see in others." (Geller, 22)

Elvis loved singing and his first memory of singing and dancing was in a church according to Larry Geller, "I'll tell you something else too, those people [in church] might be wacked out, but they know how to move. They're free. They're not afraid to move their bodies, and that's where I got it." (Geller, 40)

As mentioned earlier, critics, mostly male, tore him into pieces. He was a scapegoat for everything that was wrong on the television shows and in the movies. After all he was more popular than they were and he didn't even have their social graces or degrees. Neither did he know the right people. How could he make it to the top spot on these television programs? The world was making a big mistake. They called him "Egotistical Wonder Boy of TV," "Side-Burned Delinquent," "Pervert," "Dreamboat Groaner Elvis," "White Nigger," "Warbler," "Wicked," "Evil," and "Obscene Child."

Some claimed that his fan clubs degenerated into sexual orgies. His musical style was called "nigger music" and "devil music" by racists and fundamentalists. (*Cultural Impact*) FBI files record complaints about how he was masturbating or riding a microphone. There were even petitions circulating to ban Elvis from performing on television. Elvis complained to Marion Keisker, the woman who "found" him at Sun Records, "The only thing I can say, is that they don't know me." (Guralnick, *Last Train*, 360)

Jerry Hopkins, an early biographer, calls the following quote from *Time Magazine* one of the great put-downs of all time. "Is it a sausage? It is certainly smooth and damp looking, but who ever heard of a 172-lb sausage 6 ft. tall? Is it a Walt Disney goldfish? It has the same sort of big, soft, beautiful eyes and long, curly lashes, but who ever heard of a goldfish with sideburns? Is it a corpse? The face just hangs there, limp and white with its little drop-seat mouth, rather like Lord Byron in the wax museum." And this is only one small excerpt from the salacious indictment. (Hopkins, 160)

After his death, greedy business people in Memphis bought Elvis' original tomb when he was re-buried at

Graceland. They wanted to break it up in small parts and sell it to his fans. Their plan did not work. Their assessment of Elvis is typical of people who envied his creativity, style, and pocketbook. Their disdain reflects their own empty images of themselves. One of them said, "Elvis was the epitome of bad taste. The typical fan is a woman in her mid-thirties to forties with plastic hair, too much makeup, gaudy clothes, and a gaudy personality; a forty-hour-a-week guy who punches a clock, with a secondary education or less; people from the same social, political, and economic class he was, the lowest." (O'Neal, 36)   "No matter how successful Elvis became... he remained fundamentally disreputable in the minds of many Americans... He was the sharecropper's son in the big house, and it always showed." (*Cultural Impact*)

It is no wonder that occasional isolation became a way of coping and succeeding in his career. Although early high school friends hinted that he really did not like mixing with others who were different. Farley Guy says, "Elvis was never one to mix and mingle with strangers and neither was I. " (Burk, *Early Elvis*, 67)

Yet many were taken by his charm and wit. May Mann, a syndicated columnist, visited Elvis many times during his acting career. If you read her book, published in 1976, you realize that from the moment she met Elvis, she was in love with him. "So this is Elvis! I gasped literally, admiring his tall boyish handsomeness, his hazel eyes (which are sometimes brown and sometimes blue). What a complete surprise he is! Wow! I became momentarily like all of the millions of kids who idolize him --kids who love the escape, the happy, carefree, spontaneous laughter, who love gaiety and to feel so alone or lost." (Mann, 2) This was a "normal" reaction to Elvis and his southern manners and charm. Mann calls it "magnetic masculinity plus." (Mann, 5)

Elvis began including the "Trilogy," a southern song, on his tours in 1972. Every time I listen to it, I can see the battles, and hear the cannon fire in the background. The drums send you back in time.

An article in *Wikipedia* explains the song. "An American Trilogy" is a song arranged by country songwriter Mickey Newbury and made popular by Elvis Presley, who began including the song as part of his regular concert routine in the 1970s, thereby making the song a showstopper. It is a medley of three 19th century songs—"Dixie, a blackface minstrel song that became the unofficial anthem of the Confederacy since the Civil War; 'All My Trials,' originally a Bahamian lullaby, but closely related to African American spirituals, and well-known through folk music revivalists; and 'The Battle Hymn of the Republic,' the marching song of the Union Army during the Civil War."

Why did Elvis sing these songs? They are very

powerful songs about patriotism, religious belief, and dying for your country. They appeal to people who are serving in the military or their families because they speak of daddy dying. Of course the problems in Vietnam come to mind. Was it his way of protesting the war?

Yet, there is more. Confederate flags still fly in our country and they are not only flying in the South. We visited a state Confederate Memorial in Higginsville, Missouri not long ago. Hundreds of confederate flags were flowing in the wind. And only yesterday in the News was a piece about a group who plans to raise a rebel flag in Virginia.

Confederate Home of Missouri Cemetery

"Step lightly near this sacred spot,
*   and move with solemn tread,*
For this is consecrated soil,
*   Where sleep our honored dead!*
The sunlight shimmers through the boughs
*   Of shadowy forest trees,*
Nature weeps here, her silent tears,
*   A requiem sighs the breeze,*
When the tall grasses gently wave,
*   the wild flower lifts its head,*
As if its tribute sweet,
*   to bring to our Confederate dead,...*

                 Elizabeth Ustick McKinney, 1894

Oh so clandestinely, Elvis sings a song, "Trilogy," about his roots. It is a song of Divine triumph. "His truth is marching on." He understood the words all too well. "In Dixieland where I was born, early Lord, one frosty morn." In his own way, Elvis' career had bested the northern armies/critics. He had come from a place in the south that had no right to produce such a grand and important person.

His home of Tupelo was in Lee County, named for General Robert E. Lee of the Confederate Army. (Hopkins, 14) "To live and die in Dixie." Elvis' life became a symbol of overcoming the sorrow and humiliation of the Civil War that still devastates the South. He stood tall for his people and every person of color. At last the South had triumphed over the North with and because of their genius son.

"With everything he gave me, and with all the love, friends, memories, and music in my life --I don't ever walk alone." Jerry Schilling (Schilling, 335)

"I thought people would laugh at me. Some did, and some still are laughing, I guess." Elvis (Strausbaugh, 118)

Chapter Ten

Elvis Loved His Fans!

"It's like he came along and whispered some dream in everybody's ear, and somehow we all dreamed it." Bruce Springsteen (McDowell, 78)

"Our eyes were so dazzled with the glorious prospect set before us ... we became like the man taken out of the dark room ... the light so overpowering him that he could not see ... the idea of having one of the Godhead to reign over us was overwhelming...."

(Selvidge, *Notorious Voices*, 175.)

The second quotation above was written by a follower of Joanna Southcott during the eighteenth century. People believed that she would deliver the new Messiah. And they worshipped her. Their love for her blinded them but also invigorated them. Elvis was and is worshipped today. Marty Lacker would agree that his love for Elvis blinded him. "We thought we would die before he would. We thought he was invincible. I'd get up in a plane with Elvis, and I didn't think the plane would go down as long as he was on it." (Nash, *Mafia*, 640)

Elvis lived a myth. His music became magical for people of all ages, ethnic groups, and economic classes. He attempted to mold his life and character along the same lines of the characters in the comic books and movies. He listened to and read about the Lone Ranger, Hopalong Cassidy, Tarzan, Batman, Superman, Captain Marvel and more. (Dundy in general) When he moved to Memphis, he saw his first movie and could not take his eyes of the screen. It opened a whole world of adventure for him.

There were a lot of harrowing moments in Elvis' career when it appeared as if the fans were going to consume him, but he took the rush graciously. Some have argued that the fans imprisoned him but they were wrong. "I love the fans ... I love pretty girls. When they come running to me, I want to run to them, not away. I hope they don't blame me when Army regulations force me to look straight ahead on duty. I want them to understand I'm not ignoring them." (Mann, 9)

Perhaps the one place at Graceland where you can touch the heart of Elvis is at the wall extending around the home, called the "Wall of Love." There are so many messages on the wall that it is difficult to read them today, after all this ritual has been going on since Elvis died in 1977.

Strausbaugh captured a few of the quotes of fans, "Elvis lives in us." "There is only one king and we know who he is." "Elvis, you are my bridge over troubled waters." (Strausbaugh, 43) "My fans expect me to do the things they wish they could do--if they'd have the breaks I have.... When I'm on stage, I want to create excitement. I want each person to feel I'm performing for him or her, and even when I'm offstage, the show goes on. The clothes I wear, the cars I drive, my style of living -- they're all part of what my fans expect of me." (Esposito, 33) In 1956, Elvis employed nine secretaries to open all the fan mail. While in Germany in the Army, he received at least fifteen thousand fan letters a week." (Stone)

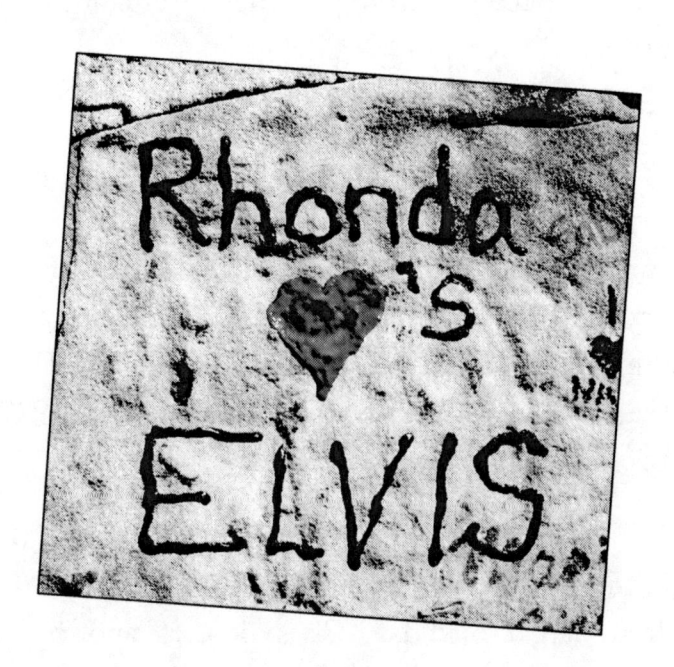

John Strausbaugh argues that there is no typical fan. "Many club founders and presidents are men, and all fan clubs assert that their memberships range across all ages, usually representing two or three generations."

(Strausbaugh, 33) Fans who follow Elvis remain forever young also. "Elvis' fans are usually stereotyped as poor white trash, working class, mostly southern, hillbillies, fat, and uneducated trailer-park housewives, etc." (Strausbaugh, 64)

If you could take a moment to analyze the above statement, you can see the arrogance and ethnocentrism of the people who concocted slander against both Elvis and his fans. Their jealousy drips from their eyes, lips, and nose because whoever they are stands on the sidelines of history.

There are millions of fans out there, and I had the privilege of meeting a few. Susanna (Sonny) is a fan who hails from Germany. She loved the movie, "G.I. Blues" that was set in Germany, and became a fan of Elvis on the day he died. Memories of standing still for one silent minute in the hallway at Central Missouri State University are seared into her mind. Since that date in 1977 Elvis has been a regular guest at her home.

For the past forty years she held birthday celebrations for Elvis and when anyone of her six children had a birthday, Elvis posters and collectibles filled the room. Elvis became her friend and she feels that Elvis lives with her. He was there for her when no one else was while she raised her children alone. She even shares Elvis photographs in the same way she would share family photos.

Her collection includes trading Elvis cards from Boxcar Enterprises (Tom Parker's Company). Besides the normal things like DVD's, books, ornaments and CD's of Elvis music, she also has two tickets to his last concert in Indianapolis. She has statues, jewelry boxes, Teddy Bears, bells, purses, wine, and so much more. When Elvis performed on television, she took photographs of him. She will never forget Elvis. Below I am including a few photos from Sonny's collection of Elvis memorabilia.

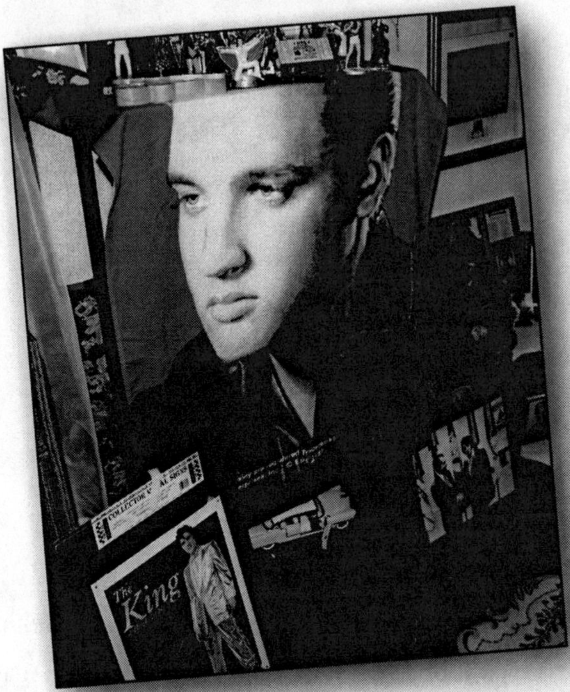
The King

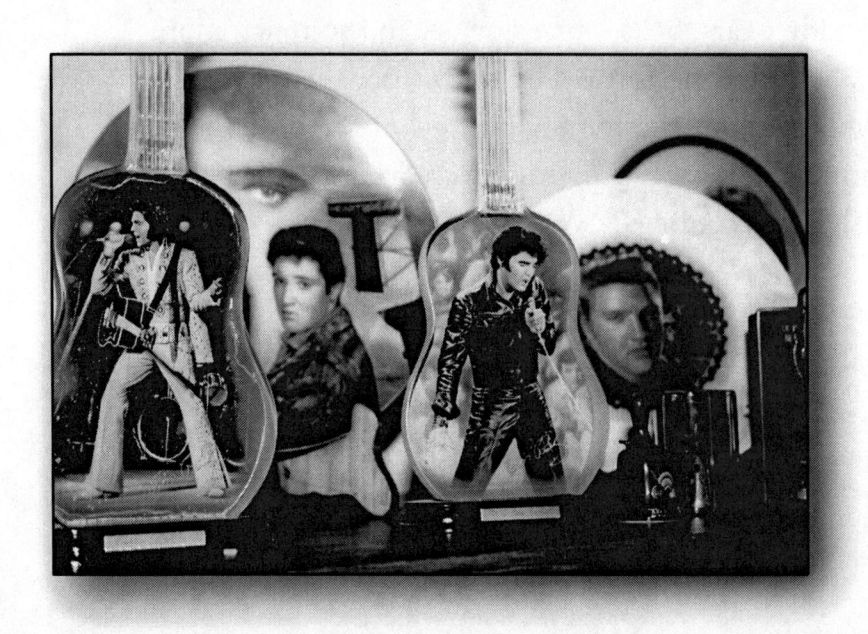

A verse in the New Testament, II Corinthians 12:15, "I will most gladly spend and be spent for your souls. If I love you more, am I to be loved less?" (NRSV) keeps bouncing in my head. The irony with many who have a great capacity for love is that others may not be able to give love back at the depth of love that was given to them. Kathy Westmoreland loved Elvis and he loved her back. "God knew what he was doing when he sent you to me. I love you, Kathy. You really do wonders for me." (Westmoreland, 116)

And if Elvis were alive today, he would send the same message to all of his fans. "I love you. You are and were my family and my life. You have made me into the person I have become. You are everything to me. My life and my music will be with you forever!"

Thank you Elvis!

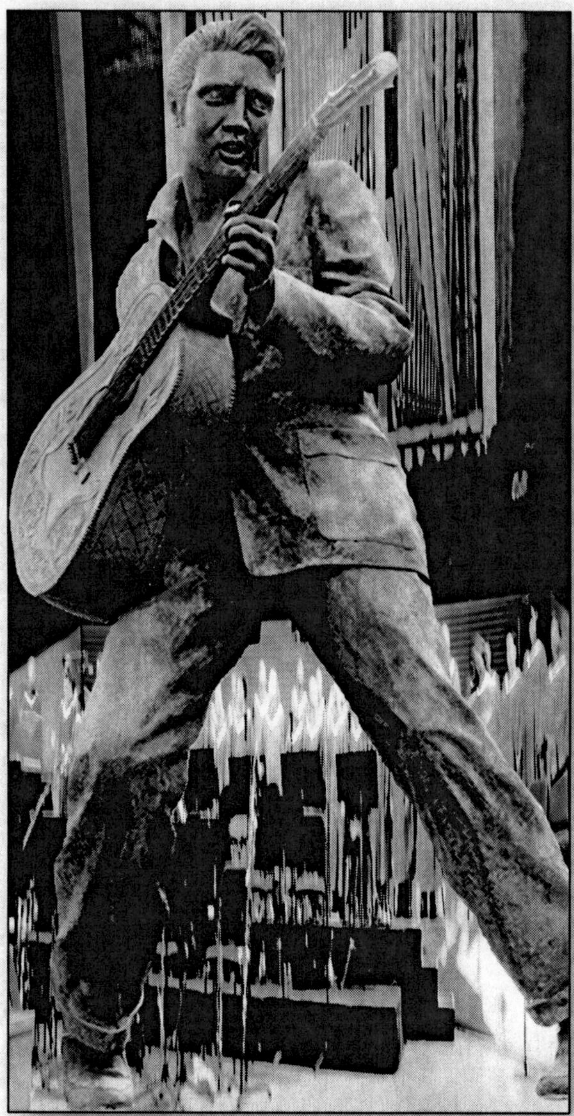

Appendix

I would like to hear your story or your thoughts about Elvis. REALLY! If you have taken unusual photographs related to Elvis, this is the place to upload them (72dpi). Remember to include an explanation of where the photo was taken and what it means to you. There is a website entitled "FortheloveofElvis" under development. Meanwhile send your thoughts about Elvis by email to Elvisloveshisfans@gmail.com or visit the blog I have created at http://selvidge.wordpress.com. Many thanks!

Selected Resources

Written Works

"An American Trilogy."
http://en.wikipedia.org/wiki/An_American_Trilogy

Arnold, Phil. "Elvis, Captain Marvel Jr. and the TCB Lightning Bolt," www.Elvisblog.net, March 31, 2012.
http://www.elvisblog.net/2012/03/31/elvis-captain-marvel-jr-and-the-tcb- lightning-bolt/

Assemblies of God USA website.
http://ag.org/top/beliefs/our_core_doctrines/

"Assemblies of God." http://en.wikipedia.org/wiki/Assemblies_of_God

"Aunt Delta." Elvisblog.net/2009/05/17aunt-delta/

Baird, Robert. "Elvis Presley. Baby What You Want Me To Do."
http://www.stereiohle.com/features/750

Bertrand, Michael T. *Race, Rock, and Roll.* Chicago: University of Illinois, 2005.

"Black Song Writers." http://www.elvis-history-blog.com/otis-blackwell.htm

Blount, Roy. "Goldman on Presley"
http:www.nytimes.com/1981/10/25/books/goldman-on-presley.html?pagewanted=all

"Bosom of Abraham, Take 3." *Elvis Presley. A Touch of Platinum. A Life in Music.* RCA, 1998.

Burk, Bill. E. Early Elvis. *The Tupelo Years.* Memphis: Propwash Press, 1994.

_____Elvis. *A Thirty-Year Chronicle.* New York: Osborne Enterprises, 1985.

_____Early Elvis. *The Humes Years*. Red Oak Press, 1990.

Chadwick, Vernon. *In Search of Elvis. Music, Race, Art, Religion*. Boulder: Westview Press, 1997.

"Charities of Elvis." http://elvis-tkc/forum2/index.php?showtopic=8848

Chuck Berry Performance.
http://www.youtube.com/watch?v=6ofD9t_sULM

Conser, Walter H and Rodger M. Payne, editors. *Southern Crossroads:Perspectives on Religion and   Cutlure*.   Kentucky. University of Kentucky, 2008.

"Counter Culture of the 1960's."
http://en.wikipedia.org/wiki/Counterculture_of_the_1960s

"Cultural Impact of Elvis Presley."
http://en.wikipedia.org/wiki/Cultural_impact_of_Elvis_Presley

DeMain, Bill, "All the King's Men. Rare stories from the band who backed Elvis Presley in his final   years." *Performing Songwriter*. Sept/October Vol 14 2006 Issue 96, pp. 20-26.

di Sabatino, David. "History of the Jesus Movement." AllSavedFreakBand.
http://www.allsavedfreakband.com/jesus_movement.htm

"Diseases of Elvis Presley."
http://elvispresleypedia.com/behind/disease.htm

Doll, Susan. *Elvis American Idol*. Calgary, Canada, 2007.

"Dolmetsch Online -Music Theory Online-Staffs, Clefs and Pitch Notation." www.dolmetsch.com/musictheory1.htm

Doss, Erika, "The Power of Elvis," *American Art*, Summer 1997, 4-7.

_____ *Elvis Culture. Fans, Faith, & Image*. Lawrence: University Press of Kansas, 1999.

Duffett, Mark. "Transcending Audience Generalizations: Consumerism Reconsidered in the Case of Elvis Presley Fans." *Popular Music and Society*. Summer 2000. Vol. 24. Issue 2. Found in Ebsco Host.

Dundy, Elaine. *Elvis and Gladys*. New York: McMillan, 1985.

Dunleavy, Steve and Red West, Sonny West, and Dave Hebler, *Elvis. What Happened?* New York: Ballentine Books, 1977.

Elms, Alan C. "A Presley Pathography." http://www.ulmus.net/ace/aceworks/presley.html

Elvis Australia. www.Elvis.comhttp://www.elvis.com.au/presley/lisa_marie_convair_880 _jet .shtml#sthash.TAHKc546.jXcQUyCK.dpbs

"Elvis Fans Greeted at Graceland by Priscilla, Lisa Marie on 35th Anniversary of Icon's death." Fan quotes. http://www.cbsnews.com/8301-207_162- 57494298/

"Elvis Festivals and Events." http://www.elvis.com/events/elvis_festivals_events.aspx

Elvis' Motorhome. www.elvispresleypedia.com/epedia/elvislife/18.htm

"Elvis Presley's Military Career." http://www.history.army.mil/fafq/elvis.htm

"Elvis Presley's National TV Appearances in the 1950's." http://www.elvis.com.au/presley/elvis_presleys_national_tv_appearances _in _the_1950s.shtml#sthash.N5SOOaqC.dpbs

Esposito, Joe. *Good Rockin' Tonight. Twenty Years on the Road and on the Town with Elvis Presley*. NewYork: Simon and Schuster, 1996.

FBI File on Elvis. http://vault.fbi.gov/Elvis%20Presley%20/Elvis%20Presley%20Part%202 %20of%2012/view

FBI File on Elvis. http://en.wikipedia.org/wiki/FBI-files_on_Elvis_Presley

Fessier, Bruce. "Director Remembers Landmark Elvis Presley Performance." Desert Sun. May 10, 2013.

Geller, Larry. *"If I can Dream," Elvis' Own Story*. New York: Simon and Schuster, 1989.

Goldman, Albert. *Elvis*. New York: McGraw Hill, 1981.

Guralnick, Peter. *Last Train to Memphis. The Rise of Elvis Presley*. New York : Little, Brown, and Co.,1994.

_____. *The Unmaking of Elvis Presley. Careless Love*. New York: Little Brown and Co., 1999.

Hodge, Charlie with Charles Goodwin, *Me'n Elvis*. Memphis: Castle Books, 1988.

Hoover, Stewart M. and Lynn Schofield Clark, *Practicing Religion in the Age of Media*. New York: Columbia, 2002.

Hopkins, Jerry. *Elvis a Biography*. California: Warner Brothers, 1971

"Interview with Red West." Elvis Australia: www.elvis.com.au. http://www.elvis.com.au/presley/interview_with_red_west.shtml#sthash.y1BsGTlq.uYjpwMfZ.dpbs

Jackson, Fleda Brown, "I Visit the Twenty-Four Hour Coin-Op Church of Elvis." *The Iowa Review* 29. 2. p. 55

Jewish Symbols. "Bar and Bat Mitzvah Gifts." *Elvis Presley News*. http://www.elvispresleynews.com/JewishElvis.html

Keene, Nick. "For the Billionth And the Last Time. Lifting the Lid on the King's Record Sales," http://www.elvisnews.com/articles.aspx/for-the-billionth-and-the-last-time--lifting-the/1126

Keogh, Pamela Clarke. *Elvis Presley. The Man. The Life. The Legend*. New York. Atria Books, 2004.

Klein, George. *Elvis. My Best Man*. New York: Crown Publishers, 2010.

Legge, Kate. "How Art and Music Therapy Help People to Recover from Tragedy and Trauma," *The Weekend Australia Magazine*. http://www.theaustralian.com.au/news/features/all-together-now/story-e6frg8h6-1226735620655

"The Lisa Marie," http://www.elvis.com.au/presley/lisa_marie_convair_880_jet.shtml#sthash. GG3eFDsz.dpbs

Lord, Lewis. "What made Elvis Wiggle?," *U.S. News and World Report*. 7/8/2002, Vol. 133, Issue 2, pp. 1-3.

"Lottery Winners." http://usnews.nbcnews.com/_news/2013/05/17/18323470-what-could-happen-to-you-tales-of-big-lottery-winners?lite

McDowell, Ronnie. *The Genuine Elvis. Photos and Untold Stories about the King*. Gretna: Pelican Publishing, 2009.

McWhirter, Cameron, "New Front in Running Battle Over Rebel Flag." *Wall Street Journal*. 9/6/13 http://online.wsj.com/news/articles/SB10001424127887323980604579030790555882238

Mann, May. *Elvis and the Colonel*. New York: Pocketbooks, 1976.

"Memphis Mafia." Wikipedia. http://en.wikipedia.org/wiki/Memphis_Mafia

Moore, Scotty. *That's Alright Elvis. The Untold Story of Elvis's First Guitarist and Manager, Scotty Moore*. New York: Shirmer Trade Books, 2005.

Moscheo, Joe. *The Gospel Side of Elvis*. New York: Center Street, 2007.

Music 354. Elvis Presley Syllabus. http://herbergeronline2.asu.edu/elvis/

Nash, Alanna. *Baby Let's Play House. Elvis Presley and the Women who Loved Him*. New York: Harpercollins, 2010.

_____ *The Colonel*. Chicago: Chicago Review Press, 2003.

_____. *Elvis Aaron Presley. Revelations from the Memphis Mafia*. New York. Harper Collins, 1995.

National Appearances of Elvis. http://www.elvis.com.au/presley/elvis_presleys_national_tv_appearances _in _the_1950s.shtml#sthash.KbiDvKMl.dpbs

O'Neal, Sean. *Elvis Inc. The Fall and Rise of the Presley Empire.* Prima Publishing, 1997.

O'Neill, Nena. *Open Marriage.* New York. M. Evans &Company, 1972.

"Otis Blackwell." http://www.elvis-history-blog.com/otis-blackwell.html

Parker, Ed. *Inside Elvis.* California: Rampart House, N.D.

Pinsky, Drew and S. Mark Young, *The Mirror Effect. How Celebrity Narcissism is Seducing America.* New York: Harper, 2009.

Presley, Priscilla Beaulieu. *Elvis and Me.* New York: Berkley Books, 1985.

"Quotes by Elvis," www.elvis.com/about-the-king/quotes/quotes_about_elvis.aspx

Reece, Gregory L. *Elvis Religion. The Cult of a King.* New York. I. B. Tauris, 2006.

"Real Good Looking Boy," en.wikipedia.org/wiki/Real-Good-Looking-Boy

Riley, Tim. *Fever: How Rock n' Roll Transformed Gender in America.* New York: Macmillan, 2005.

Robbins, Dean. "The Church of Elvis." CityView, 15. 33, p.60

"Rosetta Tharpe." http://en.wikipedia.org/wiki/Sister_Rosetta_Tharpe

Sante, Luc. "Review of Albert Goldman's Elvis." http://www.nybooks.com/articles/archives/1981/dec/17/relic/?paginati on=false

Schilling, Jerry. *Me and a Guy Named Elvis. My Lifelong Friendship with Elvis Presley.* New York: Gotham Books, 2006.

Selvidge, Marla J. *Life Everlasting* (forthcoming). See chapter on "Free Blacks."

_____. *Notorious Voices. Feminist Biblical Interpretation 1500-1920,* New York: Continuum, 1996.

"Shape Notes." http://fasola.org/introduction/note-shaptes.htm

"Signs, Symbols and Wonders,"
http://www.elvislightedcandle.org/signsymbwonders/signsymbwdrs.htm

Slade, Susan. http://voices.yahoo.com/elvis-presleys-custom-jets-tour-graceland-memphis- 659979.html

Stone, Rebecca, "50,000, 000 Elvis Fans Can't be Wrong".
http://elvisforever.tripod.com/id40.html

Strausbaugh, John. E. *Reflections on the Birth of the Elvis Faith.* New York: Blast Books, 1995.

Stromberg, Peter. "Elvis Alive? The Ideology of American Consumerism.*" Journal of Popular Culture.* Winter 1990, 24, 31 ProQuest Central.

Syllabus. Music 125 History of Rock Music. Western Nevada College.

Tharpe, Jac L. Editor. *Elvis Images and Fancies.* London: W. H. Allen & Co, 1979.

Thomas, Sally. "Grooving on Jesus," First Things 174(Jun/July 2007): 10-12

Twentieth Century Music Syllabus.
http://teachers.schoolofwestfield.org/bruno/about-2/20th- century-music-syllabus/

"Vintage Motor Homes."
http://home.comcast.net/~robmorg/oldmh/oldmh.htm

Westmoreland, Kathy. *Elvis and Kathy.* Glendale Publishing House, 1987.

Whitehead, Aaron. Book Review: "The Mirror Effect. How Celebrity Narcissism is Seducing America by Dr. Drew Pinsky and Dr. S. Mark Young," April 10, 2009 at blogcritics.org. http://blogcritics.org/book-review-the-mirror-effect-how/

Whitmer, Peter. *The Inner Elvis. A Psychological Biography of Elvis Aaron Presley.* New York: Hyperion, 1996.

Yenne, Bill. *The Field Guide to Elvis Shrines.* Los Angeles: Renaissance Books, 1999

Images

1962 Dodge Motorhome, Courtesy of Chrysler Group LLC.

Red Elvises by permission.

Sonny graciously allowed me to photograph items in her Elvis room in 2013. Thank you!

The photographer who took photos hanging on the wall in Sun Studios is not named. The owner and president of the company could not remember who took the photos.

All images are owned and copyrighted by Marla J. Selvidge and Loch Lloyd Travel Consultants LLP. Most of the images were taken or created by Marla J. Selvidge except where noted.

From Sonny's Collection of her Photos

Video Resources.

(There were too many audio resources to include here.)

"Ann Margret talks about Elvis."
http://www.youtube.com/watch?v=oRMOR8i5RMY

"Blue Hawaii." 1961, 1989 Viacome International Inc.

"Change of Habit." 2002 Universal Studios.

Charlie Hodge. "The Elvis I Knew." Decker Television and Video Productions, Inc. 1994.

"Charro." Distributed by Warner Video.

"Clambake." 1967 Metro-Goldwyn-Mayer Studies, Inc.

The Dorsey Brothers Stage Show. January 28, 1956. "Elvis-Shake, Rattle, and Roll -- Flip, Flop and Fly." Taken off YouTube. http://www.youtube.com/watch?v=cb4CCOKKh74

Ed Sullivan . September 9, 1956, "Elvis-Don't be Cruel/Love Me Tender." Taken off YouTube. http://www.youtube.com/watch?v=h-5OAKHb8LU

"Elvis." Dick Clark Productions. 1979.

"Elvis. The Mini Series." CBS Mini Series, 2007. Free on YOUTUBE.

"Elvis #1 Hit Performances." 2007. Elvis Presley Enterprises.

"Elvis #1 Hit Performances and More Volume 2." 2008. Elvis Presley Enterprises.

"Elvis. '68 Comeback Special." 1968, 1991 The Estate of Elvis Presley and Lightyear Entertainment, L.P.

"Elvis Complete. King of Rock and Roll." Special Edition. 2007 WHEUSA

"The Elvis I knew featuring Charlie Hodge." 1994 Decker Television and Video Productions.

"The Elvis Mob." ABC TV Documentary. http://www.abc.net.au/tv/documentaries/stories/s725991.htm

"Elvis on Tour." 1972 Turner Entertainment Company.

"Elvis. Rare Moments with the King." 2002 Good Times Entertainment Limited.

"Viva Las Vegas." www.youtube.com/watch?v=iNbp-mkKPCI

"Follow That Dream." 1961 Metro-Goldwyn-Mayer Studies, Inc.

Frank Sinatra and Elvis Presley, "Love Me Tender, Love Me True." http://www.youtube.com/watch?v=BskKbs_BHNg

"Frankie and Johnny." 1966 Metro-Goldwyn-Mayer Studies, Inc.

Gillian Welch, "Elvis Presley Blues." www.youtube.com/watch?v=VW8HMKk3r5Y

"He Touched Me: The Gospel Music of Elvis. http://vimeo.com/8601644

"It Happened at the World's Fair." Distributed by Warner Video.

"Jailhouse Rock." Distributed by Warner Video.

Jerry Schilling. "Jerry Schilling, friend of Memphis talks music and life at Graceland," http://www.youtube.com/watch?v=Ueew9tynAaQ

"Heartbreak Hotel" Milton Berle Show. http://www.youtube.com/watch?v=71fuhzYDeT4

"Kid Galahad." 1962 Metro-Goldwyn-Mayer Studies, Inc.

"King Creole." 1958, 1986 Viacom International Inc.

"Loving You." 1989 Good Times Home Video.

McDonald, Joe. "Feel Like I'm Fixing to Die Rag. http://www.youtube.com/watch?v=DAf_flTfobI

Janis Martin, "Barefoot Baby," and "My Boy Elvis."

"Masters of War." Song by Bob Dylan.

Merle Haggard, "From Graceland to the Promised Land."

"The Motown Effect. Short Documentary." http://www.youtube.com/watch?v=VnRfyVQS_iA

Jerry Reed, "Tupelo Mississippi Flash."
http://www.youtube.com/watch?v=aHpXYpRiwN

Dan Reeder, "Clean Elvis." http://www.youtube.com/watch?v=CxBV-nxQiXQ

Paul Simon, "Graceland."
http://www.youtube.com/watch?v=OtT7Og2LBbE

"Stay Away Joe." Distributed by Warner Video.

Tharpe, Sister Rosetta. "Up Above My Head."
http://www.youtube.com/watch?v=JeaBNAXfHfQ

"Viva Las Vegas." 1963. Distributed by Warner Video.

Wynonie Harris. "All She Wants To Do Is Rock."
http://www.youtube.com/watch?v=T_vgfavJ50E

Marla J. Selvidge, Ph.D. is Professor and Director of the Center for Religious Studies at the University of Central Missouri. She founded the Center in 1990 and has directed its growth, developing scores of courses as well as academic and public programs. Having published numerous academic books and articles, her first novel was marketed in 2013, *Demimonde. The Other Story*. Hailing from Roseville, Michigan, she has spent most of her career teaching in colleges and universities. Her Ph.D. is from Saint Louis University and the M.A. was awarded at Wheaton Graduate School. She resides with her husband, Dr. Thomas C. Hemling and two beloved canines, Charlie and Tinkerbell, in a suburb of Kansas City, Missouri. Together for over thirty years, they have traveled to at least fifty countries and plan to keep on traveling. For correspondence with Dr. Marla you can email her at selvidge@ucmo.edu

CPSIA information can be obtained at www.ICGtesting.com
Printed in the USA
LVOW11s0122030314

375753LV00003B/837/P